MINDS
MEET

Also by WALTER ABISH

Alphabetical Africa (novel)

Duel Site (poems)

MINDS
MEET

Walter Abish

A NEW DIRECTIONS BOOK

ACKNOWLEDGMENTS
Grateful acknowledgment is made to the editors and publishers of books
and magazines in which some of the material in this volume originally
appeared: *Confrontation, The Element, Extensions, Fiction, New Directions in Prose and Poetry, Paris Review, Seems, Statements: New Fiction*
(Copyright © 1975 by Fiction Collective/George Braziller), and *Tri-
Quarterly.*

The first epigraph on page iv, from "Alarm for the Year 2000" by Juan
José Arreola, included in *Confabulario and Other Inventions* (Copyright
© 1964 by Juan José Arreola), translated by George D. Schade, is reprinted
by permission of the publisher, The University of Texas (Austin). The
second epigraph is from "While Breathing" by Henri Michaux, included
in *Selected Writings* (Copyright © 1968 by New Directions Publishing
Corporation), translated by Richard Ellmann and published by New Directions Publishing Corporation.

The quotations on pages 159 and 163 are from "The Departure from
Hydra" by Kenneth Koch, included in *Thank You and Other Poems* (Copyright © 1962 by Kenneth Koch) and published by Grove Press, Inc.

Manufactured in the United States of America
First published clothbound and as New Directions Paperbook 387 in 1975
Published simultaneously in Canada by McClelland & Stewart, Inc.

Library of Congress Cataloging in Publication Data

Abish, Walter.
   Minds meet.

   (A New Directions Book)
   CONTENTS: Minds meet.—Life uniforms.—This is not a
film this is a precise act of disbelief. [etc.]
   I. Title.
PZ4.A144Mi   [PS3551.B5]   813'.5'4   74–23315
ISBN 0–8112–0557–6
ISBN 0–8112–0558–4 pbk.

New Directions Books are published for James Laughlin
by New Directions Publishing Corporation,
333 Sixth Avenue, New York 10014

To my mother and father

Watch out! Every man is a bomb about to explode. Perhaps the beloved will explode in her lover's arms. Perhaps—

Nobody can be pursued or apprehended any more. Everyone refuses to fight. In the earth's most remote corners the noise of the last unhappy mortals resounds. —JUAN JOSÉ ARREOLA

Sometimes I breathe harder and all of a sudden, with the aid of my continual absent-mindedness, the world rises with my chest. Perhaps not Africa, but big stuff. —HENRI MICHAUX

CONTENTS

Minds Meet   1

Life Uniforms   21

This Is Not a Film This Is a Precise Act of Disbelief   31

The Istanbul Papers   69

Frank's Birthday   79

With Bill in the Desert   85

The Second Leg   105

A Stake in Witches   125

More by George   133

How the Comb Gives a Fresh Meaning to the Hair   143

Crossing Friends   159

Non-Site   173

MINDS MEET

A HISTORY

The Chappe brothers were skilled technicians, and as such their
aspirations were confined to the realization of their undertaking.
They had never traveled to the heart of Mexico, and there climbed
the broad steep steps of the massive Mayan, Toltec, and Aztec
pyramids which constituted an altogether different system of communication from the one they were exploring. In France the
Chappe brothers worked around the clock perfecting the semaphore. One at a time they worked the arm that was attached to an
upright mast on the roof of their house. In those days the roofs were
slanted, and working the arm at night was extremely hazardous. In
a later version, also perfected by the Chappe brothers, the arm was
equipped with two mobile extensions, and in this form 192 signals
could be sent simultaneously, although 192 signals was a bit much
for a man to absorb at one time.

The Chappe brothers felt exhilarated when the French government under Napoleon requested that they transmit to the Dutch
the following message: Is there any other way to live? Justifiably,
the three brothers felt that they were making headway. It is not
known what the Dutch made of the message, since they never
responded to it. According to the 23rd edition of the *Encyclopedia
of the U.S.S.R.*, S.F.B. Morse, an American portrait painter, was

1

inspired to invent the Morse code after seeing an illustration of one of Chappe's semaphores in action during the siege of Condé-sur-l'Escaut, in November 1794. The illustration showed some soldiers bivouacked in a meadow a short distance from a three-story square tower that was situated on the slope of a low hill. The wood ramp and railing on the tower enabled the signal man to work the semaphore arm mounted on the roof. By no stretch of the imagination could these towers be compared to the imposing edifices built by the Pre-Columbians, but they were functional, they served a purpose, and they were inexpensive. The United States installed some in Connecticut in 1802, others along the coast of Maine in 1807, and by 1832, a network of considerable length linked Washington to the other cities in the East. Still, the most ambitious system by far was erected under Nicholas I (1825–52) when his government built stone towers at a distance of four to five miles apart, connecting St. Petersburg to Moscow. Nicholas eventually hoped to build a chain of towers to the Bering Strait, into Canada by way of Alaska, then down the west coast of the U.S. to Mexico, to the heart of the ancient empire, to the pyramids, those crumbling overgrown ruins that at one time had been Mayan signal towers, something that most archeologists had clearly failed to realize. Nicholas, at heart a resourceful romantic, wanted to plug into the Pre-Columbian system, though it is doubtful to this day whether he could pronounce the word "Tlahuizcalpentecutli," which in the Mayan language means, "Lord of the Dawn." At any rate, Nicholas's colossal undertaking can be said to rival that of Montezuma II, who prior to the arrival of Cortes was determined to discover "that which must come," only to have his astrologers, court sorcerers, and the thousands who came to the palace with their dreams put to death, because their forecasts were unacceptable.

After Nicholas's death, his son dutifully continued to pay for the upkeep and maintenance of the signal towers, although most of the messages that came pouring in from the ancient Mayans were not transmitted to Moscow, since vital sections of the line in the U.S. found it more profitable to switch to commercial messages. In some instances, subscribers were paying upward of $85 a month to be informed of a ship's arrival from Europe. As a result of this quite a number of signal men made a tidy packet and retired early. It must also be said that the majority of the signal men were Russians, which posed a problem for the U.S. Signal Corps, because the diet of the Russians was so different. Anyway, S.F.B. Morse once climbed a Mayan pyramid to get a better understanding of the system. Reaching the top he heard a babble of voices, as 3,000 years of incomprehensible history pressed down on him. Undaunted by the noise, he told the voices "to piss off." He was not concerned with history, or with the Aztec "Law of the Center." Five years later, while teaching at N.Y.U. he copied the famous experiment of Abbé Nollet, a Carthusian monk who was able to transmit an electric charge over a mile-long line of monks "who leaped simultaneously into the air and laughed heartily afterward." S.F.B. Morse, no sluggard where electricity was concerned, had the U.S. government round up all the Russian signal men, then, having handcuffed them to one another, kept them jumping for forty-eight hours. It was not a solution in communication . . . at least not for some years to come.

To this day the Mayan files are collecting dust in the archive in Moscow. An attempt had been made to translate them, and the first sentence reads: Is there any other way to live? But the Czar soon lost interest in the project, although he continued to pay for it. Some of the signal towers are still inhabited; however, only one near Dublin has received any attention in the press.

A MESSAGE

There are twenty-six letters in the alphabet. The first letter, A, resembles the twenty-second letter, V. It has a crossbar that links the two converging straight lines halfway between their ends and the point where they meet, and resembles an arrowhead pointing straight upward. The letter V, which does not have a crossbar, points in the opposite direction. Even someone unaccustomed to the alphabet will have no difficulty in distinguishing the one from the other. Arrowheads are not extinct as one might suspect. They are still painted on all sorts of directional signs, i.e., This way to the abyss, or simply MENS ROOM.

In spite of the undeniable resemblance, a person pierced by an arrow is not led to think of the letters A or V. In general, people are conditioned to think of altogether different things. Most likely in the U.S. and in other places where Western Civilization has taken a stranglehold, people think of more immediate things. They think of Ava Gardner, Errol Flynn, or Wilhelm Fürtwangler.

In some of the more backward areas in the Southwest people still use arrows. Disdainfully they shoot them into deer, and moose, and bears. In parts of New Mexico the plains are littered with arrowheads . . . From the air the ground looks like a giant alphabet soup.

The sky darkens gradually, but in spots the night sky remains brightly lit as more and more buildings go up in flames. Surprisingly no one shows any apprehension at this frequent occurrence. It is being taken for granted the way one person after another collapsing behind the checkout counter of your local supermarket from an excess of toxicity is taken for granted. Although the letters of the alphabet are independent of each other, people tend to ingest or read them, as the case may be, in small and large clusters that are called words. No matter what people say to each other, they are using words, not letters. When a word is not understood, the person using it is obliged to spell it aloud. This entails breaking the word into letters. However, if one is careful, one can speak for hours on end, even months sometimes, without once being compelled to spell a word . . . In the more rural sections of the U.S. people do not resort to spelling difficult words . . . instead they plunge a V-shaped knife into the other fella, who moans, "Ohhh." O also happens to be the fifteenth letter in the alphabet. For some reason it is often used by insecure people.

In the larger cities man's literacy is generally taken for granted. When an alarm goes out, the recipient will write on a card the location of the reported fire. The firemen are notified, and, having slid down from their living quarters on a greased pole, gather round the large wall map of their district to discuss the best approach. Many of the streets are blocked . . . many of the street signs missing . . . or pointing in the wrong direction. Still, the map is of some help. It gives the firemen a decided advantage. For one thing, all the street names are printed on the map. When a street is no longer being used, the street name is crossed out on the map. For that purpose an X, or several X's may be used. X is also the twenty-fourth letter in the alphabet. No one ever moans X, or exhales X. Only coy women will say: Although everything is predetermined, X baffled me last night by failing to decipher the message on my lips.

4

Many couples communicate with each other by leaving notes on the kitchen table. Harry comes home and reads what his wife has written. Most notes are expressly reserved for factual if somewhat prosaic statements: I have gone away, you will never see me again. The casserole is to be heated at three-fifty for half an hour. If Harry feels like it he will also write a note. On reading a note it should be possible to discover if the person writing it harbors ill feelings toward one. Frequently, for one reason or another, the author of a note may try to disguise his or her ill feelings, but like most things kept bottled up, ill feelings will out. If not in this note then surely in the next.

It is also customary for people to sign the note with their own names. They write Harry or Joe, or just initial it, H or J . . . to let the person for whom the note is intended know that they and not someone else has written it. Not infrequently the writer of notes will feel impelled to address a larger audience. He may, on his way home, stop at one of the public conveniences in the subway and write in capital letters above the urinal: Does the past leave any room for the future? The writer will have the satisfaction of knowing that many men will ponder over this question as they stand with legs apart on the brink of an incertitude that nothing will relieve.

Harry was embracing his wife when the message arrived. But they were no longer together by the time the message was deciphered a few years later. They were still avidly reading notes left for them on the kitchen table. These notes, respectively signed Bruno and Tina, helped somewhat to diminish their disquietening sense of apartness. Energetically Harry, with a compressed feeling of anguish, clipped all the articles dealing with the message from the local paper. It enabled him to recall the precise moment the message was received. To situate the exact location of their embrace, Harry tried to remember the interior of their former apartment, and while drawing its floor plan he discovered that it resembled the floor plan of his present apartment. What to do, he wondered.

In the building where Harry works, people dislike using the elevator. Quite candidly they admit to being afraid . . . As they shoot up to the thirty-third floor they shout obscenities at the operator. But all this anger does not alleviate the terror. Many unaccountably spend long hours holding their throbbing heads between their hands and crouching in a retching position. Afterward they say:

tough shit. The message did nothing to assuage people's longing and desire to come together. Harry stretched out on a mat and dreamt of impromptu sex. Now, he whispered, this second, I am ready and waiting for you. But no one rang the bell. By the time Tina entered the room ten minutes later, it was too late, decidedly too late.

Of the many divisions in the army only one is called the Big A. The men in it wear green fatigues just as the men do in the other divisions. The Big A is chiefly a useful administrative label. It is one way of having the Chiefs of Staff organize the defense of the President on paper without being plagued by tedious duplications. It also makes it possible to send one regiment to relieve another at the White House, or dig ditches for sewers . . . or do something else that is constructive.

The men of the Big A can be distinguished by their colorful shoulder patch which shows a big A on a blue background with a gold border. It's nothing fancy. There is no howling hyena on a volcano, just the letter A. The men seem to be satisfied. The patch is in the shape of a shield. The green fatigues the men wear cancel and reject all parallels that may be drawn to the age of chivalry.

The soldiers have their urinals and their beds. There is a general sort of rhythm to their everyday existence. Some have wives, others keep the names of available girls in spiral notebooks. Their needs, in other words, are taken care of. The shoulder patch unites them in a way. The letter A in this instance remains a situation. It may, for a historian who studies these matters of the heart, be a hopeless one, but how else can one keep the forest from moving in . . . how else can one prevent the stark and forbidding mountains from encroaching upon desolate cities. With a studied air of diffidence the soldiers read the message: Is there any other way to live? Over and over again.

TAKEN ABACK BY THE MESSAGE

Harry discovers Gwen in bed with Tobias and is taken aback. He says to himself, I am taken aback. His face more or less confirms this. Dubiously he inspects his face in the bathroom mirror. He is filled with a profound melancholy as well as distrust. How confusing, he thinks. Do I mistrust my melancholy, or am I melancholy because I am riddled with mistrust.

Most men feel frustrated by the time they reach thirty because there are only so many ways of making love. While the lower part of the body is actively engaged during this act of passion the face questions the veracity of its own existence. In its distress it beams all kinds of signals to the other face. These signals are by no means reliable. One might say that the faces are immersed in the self.

Tobias is a health freak. He restricts his intake of carbohydrates and teaches history at night school. It leaves him a lot of time during the day. He and Gwen share in common a love for history. He is expounding on the failure of the New Deal, while she is holding his limp prick. Harry is in five places at the same time. He is at the keyhole, in the stairwell, in the basement, passing in a bus, at work . . . Over the years his emotions have been eroded. Yet Gwen is the first to agree that Tobias is a fraud, but that doesn't prevent her from reviving his limp prick. I have discarded emotions, Tobias told her during their thirteenth bout. Emotions do not replenish me.

Harry is incensed. Losing his wife Jane, then Tina, and now Gwen to Tobias is a negligible matter compared to the deliberate assault by Tobias on his emotions. Harry stares searchingly at himself in the mirror. He is beginning to look more and more like Tobias. He strokes his new mustache and carefully straightens the black wig he is wearing. Tuesday he plans to invest in a pair of shoes with hidden lifts which will make him at least two inches taller. In this manner, he too hopes to discard emotions, and become a successful historian.

THE ABANDONED MESSAGE

Two million eight hundred and thirty-three thousand vehicles were abandoned in the countryside during the first quarter of this year. A sizable number of the abandoned cars contained people . . . some also contained pets. Of course, by the time a car is found it has already been stripped of its engine, its tires, and anything else that may be useful to another driver. In most cases the cars had run out of gas, and the driver, passengers, and pets, out of luck. Unwilling to abandon the car many people heroically stay with it.

7

Technically, as long as they remain in the car, the car cannot be considered abandoned. At one time the film industry exploited the theme of abandonment. It went to great length to build up the myth of the abandoned husband. Although some of these films were made over thirty years ago they can still be seen on television. Generally the movie's climax, if it can be called that, is reached when the wife, returning from her millionaire lover, drives her Rolls over the body of her missing husband. Bewildered they stare at each other. She accompanies him to the hospital, abandoning her car. It is not too painful, he assures her, as millions of married men bite back their tears, and their wives, in panic at their husbands' distress, welcome the oblivion into which they have sunk. Still, the word "abandoned" is rarely used in the film. In actual life it is used all too frequently; i.e., we should abandon Harlem, or we abandoned our children. Abandoned children grow up to make love like other people. But there is a sadness, a lingering wet sadness on their sallow faces as they pick up a girl on the road, and then drive their cars in circles until they have run out of gas.

To Gwen the word "abandon" is nothing new. She's familiar with the story of the abandoned little girl. Swept away by the tremendous pathos of the story, she accuses her father of turning her out. You slammed the door in my face. It was ice cold winter and you abandoned me. All I had to keep warm was a box of matches. Harry is disturbed whenever Gwen's father comes to visit, comes to plead for forgiveness. She lets him caress her small pointed breasts. His tears leave moist spots on her freshly starched dress. He's a bit daft, she tells Harry. He still thinks I am fourteen.

What are you planning to do this morning? asked Harry.

I am going to love myself and remember things . . .

As things stand there is a residue of bitterness about the message. Harry equivocates, he can't decide whether or not the 1,000-foot metal reflector at the Arecibo Ionospheric Observatory should have been destroyed. It took eight years to assemble and will take at least five years to repair. Most of the scientists were evacuated by boat to St. John in the Virgin Islands, where they spend their time drinking duty-free liquor, and making tooled leather belts. Their happy frame of mind is causing a lot of people to have second thoughts about the future destruction of scientific equipment.

Harry, sitting in his room, thoughtfully says: I can't think of anyone to abandon.

8

Some women are known to leave their apartments not later than ten each morning. They are the furtive recipients of a message. This is written all over their flushed but inscrutable faces. But no one can make out the message itself. Gwen takes a taxi to her destination. She feels quite relaxed, and even strikes up a conversation with the driver, who confesses that he has been driving past her building for the last two weeks, hoping that she would hail his cab. Nothing can undermine her confidence. She stares at the back of his large closely cropped head, and reads his unpronounceable name on the dashboard. All things being equal, she gives him a large tip, as well as her telephone number. She is sometimes given to impulsive behavior. In less than an hour she will be sipping coffee and describing her totally irresponsible action. She likes to hear herself speak. She likes to be surprised by her own words. It is spring or summer as she races up the two flights of stairs and embraces whoever answers the door. Of course, things do not always go according to plan. There's that initial awkwardness that has to be overcome, when the man keeps repeating: But who are you? What do you want? After further delays and hesitations, the man panics and locks himself in the bathroom. No amount of pounding on the door will make him open it. All this care on what to wear is thrown to the wind, Gwen tells Harry. But the next time I'll come prepared, I'll put it in print, and slip it under his door.

Abasement is located in the mind, but sometimes it is performed for the benefit of the heart. Gwen pictures herself lying in bed with the two-hundred-pound taxi driver she met the day before. I am totally independent, she says to herself. In spring or summer a woman carefully examines the moist stains on her white dress, gladly accepting a handkerchief from the first man she meets, fully aware of his complicity. I want to experience my distress in every which way, says Gwen. The stains are washed out in lukewarm water. The distress on the woman's face is only temporary. It appears to be related to the stains on her dress.

Harry reluctantly listens to Gwen describe her most recent abasement. It resembles Irma's in Tripoli. What did you do when the two-hundred-pound taxi driver followed you into the building? Gwen grimly describes the situation. Their conversation is studded with technical terms. Harry feels restless. He lights a cigarette. He

9

opens a window. He paces up and down the room. Theoretically at least half of the room is his. But which half. Left or right?

ABASHED WHILE RECEIVING THE MESSAGE

Harry is intensely sensitive to what others think of him. He is so afraid of asking the wrong question, or mispronouncing a word, that frequently he gets on a bus and rides all the way to the end of the line rather than ask the driver or one of the passengers where the bus is going. Many men, like Harry, are not certain what day of the week it is. Yet others have minds like clocks.

Harry steps into a bank in Queens and points a pistol at the bank teller. Let's have all your dough, he says. Dough, mocks the teller. What do you think this is, a bakery? Next thing you'll be asking for bread. Harry blushes furiously. He is being mocked. He feels abashed. It is a familiar quandary, so he shoots the bank teller, and then hops on the first passing bus outside the bank. Killing is a stabilizing factor in this society. But in no time Harry is again filled with a familiar panic, he doesn't know in which direction the bus is headed.

Harry undresses a woman and then undresses himself. He prolongs the undressing; he folds his trousers, his shirt, his handkerchief. He is relieved that the woman is not his wife Jane, or Tina, or Gwen, or Irma. She is someone he will not run into again. The woman cannot resist laughing when she notices the tattoo of the Mysterious Lady over his heart. Harry sees nothing funny about the tattoo. Beds also act as stabilizing factors, but not tattoos. She is still laughing when he leaves her room half an hour later. Problems between couples frequently arise . . . I'm too modest, thinks Harry bitterly, and there are gaps in my memory. I no longer remember where I met the mysterious woman of my heart.

ONCE THE KNOWLEDGE OF THE MESSAGE HAS ABATED

When a knife is pulled out of the body, the pain is said to have abated . . . although dying, too, is a form of abatement. People have a predilection for the tangible. They rest on beds, on chairs, on tree stumps, on walking sticks. Napoleon once observed that people cannot rest comfortably on their bayonets. But this remark has been taken out of context. It was lifted from a letter Napoleon wrote to his brother-in-law who had a lot of unruly people on his bayonets in Poland. In any event, where there is no room for stress, for love, for anger, there is even less room for abatement.

People everywhere study the calendar, and mark each day as it passes into a funereal darkness, out of which the next day emerges. They mark their birthdays on their calendars, and skip certain days to bring the moment of their happiness closer. The calendar is standardized . . . and no matter how one looks at it, it is a measure that encloses the apartness with all its offensive sounds. Last year on that and that day I met so and so, a woman will say to herself. I was alone as I am now . . . I smiled at him . . . I was wearing my see-through dress. My breasts were beaming messages to his eyes. Memories are also stabilizing factors. They preserve and restore as well as animate. Why else would one wish to plunder the museums? Still, memories in their random selectiveness can be said to perform a kind of abatement.

But as far as color is concerned, memory remains about as reliable as black-and-white film. Harry studiously examines the photographs of a nude at the Museum of Modern Art. He has lost all sense of time. He finds the nude engrossing, most attractive, incredibly provocative. The nude stares back at him. The museum is empty, the gates are locked, the lights are out. Somewhere in the building a guard is inserting his passkey into all kinds of elaborate electronic devices. There may even be an alert German shepherd at his heels. If all this is true, thinks Harry, then why hasn't my mind triggered the alarm system? Can it be that my mind doesn't exist?

THE ABBREVIATED MESSAGE

When the Chinese Communist Forces wish to pass for the Cooperative Commonwealth Federation, or when a physician wishes to convert his patient's conditioned reflex into a critical ratio, they abbreviate. When the dead are picked up and brought to the assembly area it is aways on CR, carrier's risk. People have been known to lose an arm or leg in transit. They are dw. Deadweight, not dustwrappers. How easy it is to shift from the intensity of one's

11

inclination which is abbreviated "I," to the moment of inertia, by simply leaving the letter "I" untouched.

THE ABERRANT MESSENGER

The bus driver presses down on the accelerator and crashes through the barricades. At night his wife Nora waits for him in bed, while he, bare-chested, smokes cigarette after cigarette. She trusts him because he is quick to respond to the insults that are heaped on her each day. She can't wait to tell him about it when he comes home. On his day off he accompanies her to the supermarket, to the drive-in bank, the swimming pool, the hairdressing salon, the bowling alley, his face flushed with indignation as she is being insulted . . .

At the motor pool he greets his friends. He's lost a lot of weight since his wife started to complain that she was being insulted. If he had not come from a poor home, he would have studied archeology, or some similar discipline. While the message is being deciphered, the bus drivers chat about their daily run. There's a grim sort of know-how in the way they lean against their buses as they wait for the word to come from Arecibo. All over the United States, bus drivers are practicing the rapid loading and unloading of their passengers. Harry passes his driving test, but the inspector is skeptical about the American flag tattooed on his hand. It looks too new.

Harry follows Nora at a safe distance. She reminds him of a bus . . . the iridescent longing on his face arouses in Nora a feeling of palpitating disgust. She waits for him at the entrance to the building. She waits for him to insult her. She invites him up to her apartment. They stand like two archaic sculptures in the room, each ready to fall at the slightest shove. I detest your hair, your nose, your caved-in chest, says Nora. But you're looking at me upside down, protests Harry. Oh, she says.

The mountains are closing in on the city . . . everyone furtively examines the pavement each day to see if it is beginning to crack. There is no way of verifying the message. It will take upward of two thousand years to receive a reply. I've slept with Jane, I've slept with Gwen, I've slept with Irma, and now I've slept with Nora, ponders Harry.

THE MESSAGE KEPT IN ABEYANCE

When an unprecedented number, three thousand, men and women plunge into a water hole in Arkansas and discover a rhino in their midst, their purpose is said to be temporarily in abeyance. In this society love slips away the moment the mail is not promptly delivered. The mailmen are past masters at this . . . they also open all the third- and fourth-class mail. They gorge themselves on manuscripts and unsolicited photographs of American Indians. By the time they get home they are saturated. Even their brains begin to reek of glue.

Nora likes to send postcards to her friends whenever she's on vacation. A restlessness drives her to seek out the Rockies. She's not afraid of earthquakes, floods, or tornadoes, since she spends the greater part of each day sheltered in the arms of the local mailman, who confides to her his bleak vision . . . and leaves her on the last day with the suggestion that she stay another week, because his friends on the night shift would like to meet her.

Everywhere people wind their watches to postpone the abeyance that threatens to overtake them. One sharpshooter on a tower can paralyze the traffic for hours. Once a bullet has entered the body, it's best to contemplate the past and not the future. The present can be said to be in a state of painful abeyance.

THE MESSAGE IS ABHORRENT

It can happen on any occasion: for instance, when visiting a friend just as he's about to garrotte his wife. To avoid the abhorrent, one must resist the persistent invitations from habitual murderers, and from people who hang outlandish looking weapons on the crimson-colored walls of the dining room.

To map the abhorrent simply follow the shrill shrieks for help. It's best to keep a pencil and a piece of paper handy. One man went down a sewer to recover his leg, only to discover that it wasn't his.

With the construction of the Great Chinese Wall, travel as we know it came to a virtual standstill. The Great Wall impeded movement . . . People resisted being walled in. They complained that their imagination was being stifled. Pole vaulting became a national pastime . . . What are we dividing with our walls, mused Harry.

We are dividing our abhorrence. Soon, as more and more walls are added, our present abhorrence will survive only as a faint memory.

What do you look like, people shout at each other across the walls. They lie about their appearance. It is pointless, really, but pole vaulting has left its scars. Their bodies follow an arc of ninety degrees in the air as they practice vaulting over the wall. No one has yet succeeded. Half the men in this country are bricklayers, the other half are dying from exhaustion. But Harry is well out of it. He has summed up his present position, but once the abhorrent has been eradicated, he plans to sum it up again.

I don't like the way you swallow your words, says Jane. I don't like the way you try to disguise your weakness by growing long sideburns, or the way you use an entire page when you sign your name in the hotel register . . . and I'm not crazy about the head-stone you picked for me.

THE ABILITY TO READ THE MESSAGE

To slide open the window and let in the cold air is to initiate an action with irreversible results. As the mind relinquishes the visual implosion, the brain cells rush items of urgent information back and forth in blind haste . . . a kind of paralysis sets in. Intention is frozen in incertitude. People are confident that they control the opening and closing of their windows . . . it imbues them with a misleading certitude that is bound to have widespread repercussions. Men think nothing of it when at night their wives ask them to shut the window. Naked they jump out of bed . . . some never make it to the window . . . some never make it back . . . Who is to measure the perils that one may encounter between bed and the opening, that rectangular opening in the wall.

A measure of man's need to survive is to be found in his pressing need for windows. Brimming over with self-confidence he stands at the window courting disaster. The man who opens other people's windows is afraid that if he would use the door he might be asked to stay for dinner. Entering through the window is an assault . . . Even though the people who live in that house or apartment may be starved for affection, they would never dare embrace the man who has soiled their linen with his boots.

Ability is a mountaintop to which people cling . . . in order to breathe the pure air, in order to give their lungs a change of pace. I'm unable to decide between him or her, says the ventriloquist. Their moans are so alike . . . but not the freshly painted windows in their room. I'm sick to death of filling puppets with voices of doom.

THE MESSAGE ABOVE

The above is chiefly referred to by people who are familiar with the below. The skywriter, like you and me, enjoys an occasional chat with his neighbor's wife. In marked contrast, horses and collectors of rare china weave back and forth with delicate, almost prissy motions. Their exercises show a kind of refinement, a result of in-breeding . . . Horses are kept in houses that are called stables, and mostly, with rare exceptions, breed only with their own kind. Collectors channel their furious energy into collecting . . . they have been known to abstain from sexual intercourse out of a desire not to spread their beautiful glaze.

When a pilot flies upside down, the above seeks to pull him below. The subject of the above is broached in most of the literature of the antiquities. It has also marked the American sensibility. I'm not above sleeping with my friend's wife, Tobias tells Harry. In Minnesota twenty thousand people gathered in the main square and watched Tobias as he demonstrated the toy helicopter. Hallelujah, they cried, as he stayed aloft for over two hours.

THE MESSAGE IS ABSENT

The messenger wears a clean shirt, but the grime is visible under his nails . . . The sky is a dull grey, but farther out, only a few hundred miles away, it is a Mediterranean blue. Everyone evokes its blue absence . . . People indiscriminately speak about each other's tragedies . . . they speak about them in an almost flippant manner so as not to be carried away by the imminence of the startling discovery that they are totally immune to the burning house next door, and have no further need to disguise their diffidence. So the absent is a solution . . . If the house next door is not burning, so much the better . . . The messenger spotted the two men in leather jackets waiting for him in the hallway. He stopped. He hesitated. He raced back upstairs, they in hot pursuit. He ran past the doors, the closed doors with the familiar numbers: 5a, 5b, 5c, 5d, 6a, 6b, 6c, 6d, 7a . . . but there was no seventh floor. Everything that is not here is absent. The only thing that is not absent, said the policeman's wife, is lust. May I, asked the messenger, unbuttoning her blouse. He had a clean shirt on, she said afterward, justifying her amorous response, a response that had been all out of proportion to his.

In this humdrum life so many encounters lack the specificity of a stain. Everywhere the housewife looks there is lust staring back at her. It is cold clinical lust, compressed into a can of shaving soap. She stares at it fixedly. One day she will cover herself with it.

The dockworkers assemble each day at the pier. They say "present" when their names are called. They all have strong emotional fathers . . . They have daughters who have learned to say: That's wonderful to hear. The men are unpacking crates that contain machinery from Japan. The message on their muscles bulges with a fierce hunger, an unreliable hunger that will settle like a wave, like a terrific squall over the upturned faces of the young men on Christopher Street.

The policeman on the beat calls the men by their first name. He calls them Archibald and Turnpike . . . but the distance between the men and him cannot be bridged so easily. They refuse to acknowledge his authority, which is enough to keep them apart. The policeman's wife confuses all messages with lust. All that is not lust is absent. Their son is a mailman. One day he hopes to deliver the mail to the White House and screw the President's wife.

When the people are absent in the early morning hours, each sound is accentuated, exaggerated . . . each sound is being rehearsed for a later occasion . . . People absent themselves behind closed doors after hearing or reading the message: Is there any other way to live? They cloister themselves in small rooms with lousy smells and nervously munch biscuits.

Everything that happens a second time is unbearably familiar, except for the trip through the tunnel. People still tolerate the trip because it breaks the monotony of the sunshine. They remain inside their cars and think.

When my parents went dancing, said the policeman's son to Harry, I was absent. I yelled to them not to leave me, but they didn't hear me, or worse yet, they pretended not to hear me. Now I must have the President's wife.

Harry has finally destroyed his play. It ran to eight hours with only two brief intermissions. All of the main characters, who resemble Harry in appearance, died either from suffocation, strangulation, or knife wounds. Harry had spent five long years working on the drama . . . he worried and brooded a lot. There was a certain satisfaction in destroying the play, the satisfaction people take when they cut off a finger. Good riddance . . . now I'll have fewer hangnails. It is the second drama Harry has destroyed. How many dramas does a man have in him?

The next day Harry started on a new play. It was about a man who jumped into the river to save another man from drowning. The man who jumped in resembled Harry, so did the man who was drowning. Neither knew how to swim. When both were fished out of the river, Harry's protagonist jumped in again. The first time, Harry reasons, he intended to save the drowning man. But the second time?

The play can be said to be about Harry and the Hudson River. Of course, to some extent it also included the barges that are towed up and down the river. It was unavoidable that Harry would include the barges. He had such a warm feeling toward them. He started the play with one objective in mind: that it be a happy play. He avoided using the word "abstain." There's no profit to be found in its use. It is droll, said Gwen, that Harry's play revolves around the river. The characters in the play fall into stereotypes: the dramatic Harry, the serious Harry, the miserly Harry, the recalcitrant Harry, the other Harry who is a buffoon, and the melancholy tugboat captain. Everyone who read the play was touched in some manner or form by its bathos. They could not help but pity Harry, and permitted him, this once . . . just one time, so that he would know what ecstasy was like . . . But Harry kept on being troubled by the inequities that made some people happier than others.

One day he met two friends from Minneapolis who were visiting the city. They urged him to accompany them to a whorehouse. At first he was reluctant to go, because it seemed such a tourist thing to do. But finally he agreed. He envisioned fantastic draperies and a marble staircase, and tall women with poodles on the leash. But there were no fancy draperies, no marble staircase, and no poodles. Filled with regret he and his two friends wandered over to a tattoo

17

parlor. Now, at last, the mysterious woman of his dreams would be close to his heart, thought Harry.

THE MESSAGE COMES APART

What about those notches that men make on their combs now that guns have been outlawed? The habitual desire to possess another man's wife is regretfully abandoned, but not the need to add the number of hours spent waiting for her in a hotel. The mileage brings us closer, says the mechanic at Gulf. So people dutifully add the mileage. How many miles have you come together? asks the Shell service attendant. We have come apart, softly replies Gwen.

People urgently whisper their name to strangers, and ask themselves: Will we do it again? Somehow the furtive element cannot be removed from the exegesis of love. The furtive lover is sustained by the number of self-inflicted scratches on his face. Harry agrees with Tobias that Gwen is a cut above the ordinary . . .

While browsing in a bookstore, Harry noticed two heavy-set men with beards whispering behind the counter. Two years later he spotted them in a grocery store on 89th Street. This time they were clean shaven. They were buying fruit. They were appraising each apple as if it were a freshly mined diamond. Harry looked at them closely but could not tell them apart. A year later, while traveling through the Florida swamps, he came across them again. They had pitched their tent in a small clearing. They also had a fire going. One of the men was kneeling beside his companion who lay stretched out on the ground. Harry did not know that the prostrate man was dead until he was quite close to the tent. Who are you? he finally managed to ask the kneeling man. The memory of that moment is forever stamped on his mind. Now, I am the survivor, whispered the man.

AN AUSPICIOUS MESSAGE

The universal reaction to the auspicious is to render it useless. The first ten minutes of a film may be considered auspicious if a fist is clenched. As the narration unfolds, a horse is casually put out of its misery. It slumps to the ground, pinning the rider against a bed of roses. The audience remain rooted to their seats. Here and there a few hesitantly push their clenched fists into the air. At times the sky turns a bright orange. An auspicious sign for someone setting off for an unknown destination. A year later the explorer returns, and there is one less unknown place to visit.

In small lofts located in cast-iron buildings metal rods are being manufactured that will play a significant role when the auspicious moment arrives, although no one can tell what form that moment will take. The two musically gifted lovers do not wait for the auspicious moment as they set out to visit an aging aunt. They are all smiles as they ride to the station. The young man is the first to dismount. It is one of those incendiary moments when all of life is on the brink of a new discovery. The zip on his pants has burst open, and despite all desperate and feverish attempts refuses to close again. She felt a sudden relief as he, this pink-cheeked lover of hers, rather than face her in this crisis, stepped in the path of the oncoming train. The auspicious exaggerates . . . it adds another dimension to one's measured reliance upon messages.

LIFE UNIFORMS
A Study in Ecstasy

I've come to depend on Arthur more than I care to admit. Almost daily we discuss the most recent disaster. Almost daily we also discuss Mildred. I enjoy talking about Mildred. Arthur has a probing mind. A relentless mind. He is not convinced that I understand Mildred. He wishes to broaden my understanding. In a sense the people he brings to the apartment are there for that purpose. To broaden my understanding. Arthur has also mapped most of the unsafe buildings in the business district for my benefit. I do my best to avoid them. Some weeks as many as three buildings collapse in a single day. Because of the alarming rate at which buildings are caving in, it may take a year or longer before the rubble is cleared away and the site is turned into another parking lot, an amusement park, or simply left vacant. Still, the high mounds of rubble have little effect on the people. Life seems unchanged. There is, however, a certain broadening understanding since Arthur was hired by one of the city agencies to document these disasters. By now, determining which building will disintegrate next has turned into a fine science. Some of the best minds sit in a room in City Hall and feed facts into a computer. Once agreement has been reached on a site, Arthur is sent to photograph it. He uses an old German camera. Sometimes the camera is mounted on a tripod. Quite a few of the photographs Arthur takes make the front page of *The New York Times*. It is a grim business.

I met Arthur as he was focusing his Leica on the building I was about to enter. I hadn't noticed the thin cracks in the wall . . . those ominous cracks. Hold it, he shouted. Somehow the urgent note in his voice made me stop in my tracks. Less than a minute later the fourteen-story building caved in. Almost gently, floor by floor, it lowered itself to the ground, while raising a huge cloud of dust. A few people jumped out of windows. Arthur kept taking photographs. I never interfere with the larger scope of things, he later explained. You stopped me in time, I reminded him. But I recognized your face, he said.

The people at the electric company do not visit the disaster sites. They have no need to. They can tell what happened from merely looking at their instrument panel. They can determine the number of kilowatt-paying customers they lost on each floor, as the needles on the instrument panel flicker. There's much to be said for electricity.

I carefully screwed the 200-watt lightbulb into the socket. I did it on the advice of Arthur. I did it also to better illuminate what I was doing. In the past year Arthur had lived in eight different locations. That kind of experience is not to be dismissed lightly. Structurally, he said, the building in which I was staying seemed sound. He pounded on the floor with a stick to demonstrate its soundness. However, the elevator was too slow in responding, and the lighting was inadequate. Personally, being aware of the trouble the electric company had taken to bring electricity to this building, and above all to this apartment, I was less critical of their somewhat sluggish performance. After all, the work had entailed laying miles and miles of electric cables, most of them underground. Hundreds and hundreds of man hours. I kept thinking of those hundreds of man hours spent laying cables. All the same, following Arthur's advice, I did not inform them that I had screwed a 200-watt lightbulb into the fixture. It was quite conceivable that the socket was not made to carry anything as large as a 200-watt lightbulb. There may be something written on the socket to that effect. The man who comes to read the meter was here this morning. My heart was pounding as he stood beneath the 200-watt lightbulb. He glanced fleetingly at the most recent enlargement of Mildred. Except for the pile of photographs on the table, the table was bare, since I was afraid that any additional weight might be too much for it to support. How did I arrive at such a conclusion. Years of experience, that's how. The meter man briefly rested his flashlight and ledger in which he entered the kilowatt-hours on a conveniently closeby chair, and studied the ecstatic expression on the topmost photograph. I had not invited him to do so. But given the bareness of the table, the photograph on top of the pile was extremely conspicuous. Gravely, for a few seconds the meter man focused his full attention on the ecstatic expression of Mildred. He struggled with some undefinable emotion, but finally left rather abruptly without saying a word. I can understand his difficulty. His training had not prepared him for such an eventuality.

Everyone who has seen Mildred under the glare of a 200-watt lightbulb has found the information Arthur has been able to elicit from her most appealing. Everyone was quick to agree that Mildred had a pair of marvelous legs. White sensuous legs. Needless to say, Mildred is not completely unaware of the effect her legs are having on some of the occupants of this apartment. Similarly I was given to understand that her husband, Mr. E. Batch, is not totally unaware of their effect either. However, he doesn't have a single 200-watt lightbulb burning in their home. This deficiency is further aggravated by his lack of awareness regarding the existence of this remarkable group of photographs. When he does hear of it, it will doubtlessly come as somewhat of a surprise. Still, he will be gratified that none other than his wife Mildred had been chosen for this study.

Mr. Batch works in an office in the city. From his desk he can see an occasional cloud of dust envelop a tall building. Much time is wasted in the office by everyone standing at a window watching the tall and by now familiar-shaped columns of dust that after an hour subside, revealing a fresh vacuum. Mr. Batch believes everything Mildred tells him. Perhaps he believes her out of a fear of what might happen if he failed to do so. But that is hypothetical. He believes that Mildred has a close friend named Paula who lives in an apartment building that is located less than ten blocks away. He doesn't know Paula's second name. He has never bothered to inquire. Mildred, I believe, married Mr. Batch because he is industrious and because he does not ask too many questions. His questions are reserved for dinner. Why aren't we having any veal cutlets, he might ask her. Although it does strain his credulity, after all he is not a complete ass, Mr. Batch believes that his wife visits her friend Paula at least four times a week. You are seeing a lot of her, aren't you, he once remarked. In the evening Mildred gets on the phone to Paula, and in his presence refers at great length to her visit that afternoon. Of course Mr. Batch cannot be certain that it is Paula on the other end of the line. Even if he spoke to Paula he could not be certain since he's never met her. What is she like, he once asked Mildred. Paula loves anything to do with literature. Paula is dark and has a Slavic accent, said Mildred firmly. Mildred's firmness is a wall erected by her to prevent Mr. Batch from casually exploring the inner recesses of her daily pleasure.

In the electric company an employee jots down on a chart that I have broken a company rule by screwing a 200-watt lightbulb into a socket that was not designed for 200-watt lightbulbs. It will be some time before the electric company can take any action. They have other concerns, other priorities that are sure to delay any action they may take. Although, in a sense, one can say that the action has already begun with the notation on the chart. The coded notation by itself appears perfectly harmless. It may be nothing more than a checkmark. The absence of windows in the electric company prevents the employees from seeing the rising and subsiding clouds of dust. Everyone has more time to concentrate on the paperwork. The information that exists on paper is not necessarily conveyed by word of mouth, but carried by a messenger. He carries the checkmark to a secretary. The secretary who is seated at a gleaming Formica table doesn't know my name. She types it without properly looking at it. On the windowless walls are large calendars with reproductions of attractive foreign landscapes. Nowhere is there the slightest indication of a cloud of dust.

The secretary who is typing my name is using an IBM electric typewriter with an eighteen-inch carriage. She sits on a swivel chair. Industriously she is utilizing the electric typewriter with the full co-operation of the electric company. They even know when her slender and quite graceful fingers are pressing the letters on the keyboard, but they do not know what letter she is pressing at any given moment. If she were to press the same letter over and over again, none of the men who are responsible for feeding the electricity into the wires would be the wiser. They are not oblivious of her fingers. Her fingers have a certain hold over them. It is an innately satisfying hold. Like most men they are receptive to certain letters. One might say that they respond more quickly to specific letters. In most instances they prefer the letter F. Fruitful, fancy, and forlorn are only three of the several hundred combinations racing through their minds. Still it can be said that their F preference is a common preference. It is, one thing remains sure, a preference uniting the men who splice the cables, and the man who reads the meter, and the elevator operator in my building. All are practitioners of F. F is a factor in their life, as it is in mine. All the same, unlike them I never use the elevator because it is unsafe, and one rides up and down at one's own risk. These are the words of the management. As the elevator rises the risk increases.

Who are all these men, asks Mildred as she enters the apartment. She sits on my chair without once thinking that at some point in time the legs might give way. She lies on my couch with the same disregard for danger. The letter F rears itself in her head as well. Frequently she substitutes another letter for F out of a misplaced sense of propriety. Yet the letter F is visible on the enlargements. It is visible when she crosses her legs, which she does frequently.

What does Mildred do when she's not visiting us, asks Arthur.

Arthur secretly uses an electric shaver. To confuse the electric company, he switches off every thirty seconds. Since it is not my shaver, I've not informed the electric company about it. They have their doubts. They have gone over the list of all my electrical appliances. Those thirty second spurts of electrical activity continue to confound them. They cannot determine what is causing them.

I have lived all my life in the city. Most worthwhile efforts take place in the city. An indescribable alertness divides the people who live in the city from the people who live in the country. Mildred is a city person. She takes the elevator to the sixth floor. The absence of large tracts of freshly plowed earth does not upset her.

Who are all those men in your apartment, asked Mildred breathlessly. Who are all those men? They're friends of Arthur, I said. When your hand touches me, she said, I break out in goose pimples all over. I took a certain satisfaction in hearing that. I knew that Arthur and his friends must have heard it too.

When I'm not working in the darkroom I am examining my next move. I know my next move may well depend on those guys at the electric company. What made Mildred say: As soon as you opened the door, I wanted to glide into your arms. Is that statement consistent with what I see on the enlargements. I enlarge Mildred. It is work that fills me with a private satisfaction. It is quite gratifying. Enlarging Mildred the better to see her F stop. Everyone who enters stares expectantly at the enlargements on the table. They seem to know intuitively that the woman in each of the photographs is Mildred. They seem to know that the slight smudge on one was caused by my hand. This hand has caressed every inch of the eleven-by-fourteen paper, I tell Arthur and his friends. In the darkroom this hand is always protected by a rubber glove. The lengths of the exposures are listed in my notebook. The notes represent years of study. They represent a boundless energy and an acute vision.

The doors on either side of my desk are always open. I'm inclined to believe that they can no longer be closed. But I don't wish to subject them to that test. Open as they are, they disclose another brightly illuminated space. The threshold I have noted in my notebook functions as a kind of boundary or frame. Sometimes I cross that frame. Sometimes I find a reason to cross the boundary. Had the door not been opened I would have been compelled to knock or to rattle the doorknob. When Mildred lies down on the couch in the adjacent room I can observe her from where I am sitting. I cannot see her when I am in the darkroom. She knows this. Arthur and the others know this. No one has ever tried to close the door in my face. It would be inconsiderate, this, after all, being my apartment.

I received the invitation to lecture at the Felt Forum by mail. The invitation, couched in the appropriate polite form, was contained in a legal-sized envelope. Most messages arrive in envelopes. Most are dropped in my mailbox downstairs. If I scrutinize the mailman when he delivers the mail, it is not done to embarrass him. It is done to elicit some kind of information. . . The mailman once delivered a package to my door. I did not invite him in. Whenever I look at him I feel that he has not forgiven me for not inviting him into my apartment and showing him Mildred's photograph.

If I am constantly conducting myself with a certain indisputable authority it is because I am describing a phenomenon that is still new. In time the newness will wear off. In the next room a woman is undressing. I can see her quite clearly. Her every gesture is studied. She looks familiar. I have seen her quite frequently. She seems to be deriving a certain pleasure from her present activity. She has a striking figure. The men are also familiar. Only this morning I had a lengthy conversation with one of them. They all appear to show a complete disregard for their safety by wrestling on the bed, despite the creaking floor. Notwithstanding Arthur's assurance, the floor could cave in at any moment. The 200-watt lightbulb illuminates the men as they one by one evoke a look of startled recognition on the woman's face . . . the look seems to say: Ahh . . . here it comes again . . . the familiar ecstasy.

The combination of the chlorine and the iodine vapor has greatly increased the sensitivity of the photographic plate. For the first time her emotions could be clearly assessed on the enlargement, but now the process took much longer. Still, I felt it was definitely worth the effort . . . all those weeks spent in the darkroom. It had taken me two years to produce the plate of Mildred. I now somewhat regretted having used Mildred instead of Muriel, because Muriel was less outgoing and more resistant to pleasure, consequently the evaluation of her troubled mind would have been more difficult, and as a result my work would have been more satisfying. After all, the conclusions I was able to draw from Mildred's photograph did not radically differ from what I had been told about her. All the same, correctly interpreting Mildred's uninhibited acceptance of F enabled me to eliminate much of the guesswork in the darkroom. The next plate, I surmised, should not take more than six months, one year at the most.

Let us now consider the world open to us, said Mildred in the adjacent room as one by one the men parted her glorious legs. In the beginning the long U-shaped corridors outside had completely disoriented them. They had lost their sense of direction as they stared at Mildred.

All this time Mr. E. Batch does not suspect a thing. The white legs that had given me so much trouble in the darkroom were now firmly locked around Arthur's obese body . . . a certain trembling motion was to be detected with the naked eye. The motion improved the shape of their bodies, I decided, since the few minor flaws became less and less evident.

What did you do this afternoon, asks Mr. Batch. Seemingly unperturbed, she crosses her legs. Mr. Batch looks at her legs. In the newspaper he has read that a certain lecture will be given at the Felt Forum, and that there is a sense of great expectation amongst the foremost scientists and amateur photographers. Mr. Batch marvels at everything Mildred says. He marvels at her excellent taste whenever she buys herself a dress. He also marvels that she had married him.

You are my developer, she says, and he beams happily.

Poor Mr. Batch.

When I entered the large hall of the Felt Forum I was greeted by a standing ovation. With quick steps I made my way to the stage, holding Mildred's photographic plate in one hand. I had, as a matter of fact, anticipated the applause, and kept my gaze fixed straight ahead as I walked to the center of the stage. It was a Tuesday, and it wasn't raining. From the amount of applause I could only assume that the hall was filled to capacity. If Arthur was to be trusted, the Felt Forum was in no immediate danger of collapsing. Somewhere among all those people waiting to hear my lecture was a face I was bound to recognize. I had taken the escalator to the second floor. It was not the first time that I had used an escalator. Naturally I am somewhat intrigued by every innovative mechanical breakthrough. A slow-moving staircase. Quite ingenious. In everything that is powered by electricity I see a future use that can be applied to my photographic explorations. Somewhere in the days ahead I might well utilize the escalator. In the first row sat a very attractive woman. She resembled Mildred. When I took another look at her I realized it was Mildred. I knew so much about her. I could only assume that the man sitting stiffly at her side was Mr. Batch.

The entire world is now open to us, I told a hushed audience.

Mildred's husband has a neat and well-groomed mustache. The information available to him at this stage can be said to encapsulate his love for Mildred and his need to be punctual. Every question he has ever asked has been answered to his satisfaction. There are 1,855 seats in the hall, and all were occupied. He and his wife occupy two seats in the first row. He has questioned Mildred about the seats. The front-row seats seem a trifle conspicuous to him. In the past his seating experience has been a more modest one. How did you manage to get two seats in the first row, he asked Mildred.

She crosses her legs.

She also stood up frequently in order to see everyone seated behind them. Her white teeth are very much in evidence. She is smiling at the entire world.

Why on earth are you standing, asked her husband.

I'm looking for Paula.

Paula. I didn't know that Paula was coming.

Mildred wore a red suit. It was a bright red, and when she stood everyone could see her clearly, although the suit obscured certain details of her body that could be seen on the enlargements.

As soon as electricity was discovered, the electric company was formed, I said. One of their first actions was to rush a wire to my darkroom.

Why aren't you more pleased with your success, asked a colleague afterward.

Basically I think that Mr. Batch pushes his admiration for Mildred too far. He doesn't even know that certain words he uses at night are now defunct.

Arthur shaved carefully before leaving the apartment at six. Feeling an uncontrollable yearning for F he made a pass at Muriel. She removed her false eyelashes before calmly stabbing him in the palm with a carving knife she carried in her purse. He was transfixed with surprise. Since this happened on the escalator, he disappeared from sight at the top of the second floor. Muriel in a state of shock rushed to the well-lit powder room. Luckily her purse also contained the fourth volume of the *Encyclopaedia Britannica*. She looked up "Fucking." It was sandwiched between "Fuchsin" and "Fucoid." It was the right book for an emergency. This could not have happened before the advent of electricity and modern photography.

I still can't get over Muriel's legs, said Arthur when he returned to the apartment, his right hand in a sling. They remind me, he said, of my recent trip to Ireland. The white legs of Ireland.

When I addressed a gathering of 1,855 scientists and photographers at the Felt Forum, the photographic plate was on the lectern, but when I returned after a ten-minute intermission it had vanished. Two years of research thrown to the wind. But two hours later I experienced my first erection in years. What a relief. I rushed to a phone, but Mildred and Mr. Batch had left for Switzerland. I think you need a new pair of pants, said Muriel when she saw me . . .

Dear Muriel. It's either that or . . .

Or what, she asks as she rushes into my arms.

THIS IS NOT A FILM THIS IS A PRECISE ACT OF DISBELIEF

PART ONE

1

This is a familiar world. It is a world crowded with familiar faces and events. Thanks to language the brain can digest, piece by piece, what has occurred and what may yet occur. It is never at a loss for the word that signifies what is happening this instant. In Mrs. Ite's brain the interior of her large house with a view of the garden and the lake are surfaces of the familiar. She is slim, and moves quite gracefully from one familiar interior to the next. Her movements are impelled by familiar needs. Each time a door is swung open or shut, it indicates that the realization of some need is under way. The needs change from moment to moment. To some degree the objects in the familiar interior of her house channel the needs. Mrs. Ite divides her time between the upstairs and the downstairs, between the inside and the outside. However, the gardener trimming the hedges is not concerned with Mrs. Ite's needs. But insofar as he is mowing the lawn, or trimming the hedges, he is satisfying at least one of them.

Three years ago Mrs. Ite walked through her familiar world and found that something was definitely missing. She knew it was something very familiar, something that was at home among the familiar setting of her furniture. That's really odd, she said to her son Bud. Something seems to be missing from our interior. Well, said Bud, after a quick look around, it can't be anything terribly familiar.

2

Michel Bontemps arrives in a place that may not yet exist. He is carrying a dictionary, he is wearing a pair of dark sunglasses, he is quite erroneously, it turns out, expecting a large reception. He has been in America once before, and the difficulties of the past can now, to his mind, be avoided. In place of the past difficulties there will be other difficulties. He is not alone, but has brought along a couple of young assistants . . . they also happen to be his close and intimate friends . . . at least that is how he refers to them, and that is how he is pleased to think of them. But largely because of his past experiences he can't bring himself to trust them. It can be said categorically that all the friends of his past are no longer his friends. Quite a number have written accounts of their friendship with Bontemps. They have paid great, perhaps excessive attention to his dark sunglasses, his fifteen innovative films, his occasional temper tantrums, his marriages, his boat mishap, as well as the interior of his apartment (in each account, needless to say, a different apartment is being described), and the way he chooses to arrange the furniture and thereby create a topography for his daily needs. By and large his needs are familiar. But Bontemps, who has read the accounts of his former friends, disagrees with their assessment, for implicit in what they have written is an attempt to define and understand the singularity of his needs. From reading any one of these accounts one may be led to believe that to rely on his close friends is and will forever remain Bontemps's priority. To see this in print is faintly distressing to him. He is torn between confiding his needs and ideas to his assistants, of whom, at this moment, there are two, and keeping his mouth shut. By keeping his mouth tightly shut he is, of course, depriving his admirers of the information they need to sustain their belief in the uniqueness of his vision. At this very moment he is landing in a familiar landscape. Both the sky, which is a clear and deep blue with patches here and there of low-lying clouds, and the hills in the distance, which to his eyes seem to be covered by a thick dark green foliage, could have appeared in any of his later films that were shot in color. If to him the landscape looked uncommonly familiar, it looked familiar because it or its exact replica has, he remained convinced, appeared in some of his films. By seeing, or rather, by recognizing the landscape he was able to savor, such is the ability of the brain, the particular sequence marked by the landscape in his films, and to recall everything that preceded and followed that appearance.

Everyone meeting Bontemps immediately wonders about his relationship to his two assistants. Michel Bontemps said to me before we left France, I hope you will have the good sense not to put on paper every word I utter. Bontemps's most recent films have all been shot in color. Every single object on the screen has a color by which it can be identified, yet somehow the color, intentionally or not, by its very explicitness, by its unambiguousness, intensifies the meaning of every object, thereby creating a curious aesthetic of shapes and colors that diminish the meaningfulness of the actions undertaken by his characters. Actions become patterns of color. I do not quarrel with Michel over his use of color. I do not quarrel with Michel for painting purple the tub in which the protagonist in Michel's most recent film is shot by his wife as he is taking a bath. Did the purple heighten or diminish the effect of a partially submerged body being shot at close range three or four times. Since this particular act could not, by any stretch of the imagination, be considered a revolutionary act, it is of no concern to me.

The three of us share one hotel room. We also share the familiar surfaces of our surroundings and the sensations we are able to derive from these surroundings. We share one double bed, and twice daily brush our teeth with a substance that is squeezed from a tube, each one of us leaving the imprint of his or her fingers on the tube until that imprint is altered by the next user. Sometimes I put on Michel's hat or pants, and sometimes he wears my shoes. There is no way I can possibly express the intense love, friendship, and admiration I have for Jill and Michel. I have confided to Jill my fear that his exaggerated and excessive use on the screen of strong blocks of color will detract from the single-mindedness of our revolutionary intent. After our arrival I extracted from Jill the promise that she will not sleep with him without first letting me know. Casually she undresses in our presence . . . naked she sits on the bed as Michel and I discuss the needs that color our daily life . . . Since neither Jill or Michel speak English they are, to a degree, dependent on me. I don't object when Michel keeps handing Jill books to read. He is educating her . . . he is preparing her for the needs made implicit in his recent films. He needs me, she says trustingly.

3

Mr. Cas Ite designed the Mall on Route 11. Route 11 is a busy highway that connects the two large towns. There was a detailed description of the Mall in one of the Paris dailies. The article claimed, among other things, that the Mall was large enough to accommodate the needs of the two towns that were fourteen miles apart. The Mall's architect anticipated that a good many of the small stores in both towns would go bankrupt in a year or two. I brought the article to Michel's attention. But by now he has forgotten that detail. The Mall at present exists in a kind of no man's land that, I know, has a special attraction to Michel. Initially Mr. Ite was worried that the unattractive windowless exterior would ruin his reputation. What would his colleagues say. Screw them, said Mrs. Ite. Build the Mall. It will be good for you. You can always add an indoor fountain and piped-in music to make it more cheerful. And it is true, the fountain and the music may delay the inevitable discontent, just as Bontemps's films accelerate it.

Michel speaks of renting the village of South Tug, which is only a twenty-minute walk from Route 11 and the new Mall. If possible I'd like to destroy some of the buildings, says Bontemps, chop down some of those tall elms, and wreck a few cars. He is planning his approach to the Mall . . . He hasn't even seen the area. He is working from a map on which the Mall, the Museum of Need as he refers to it, is circled in red.

I am told by everyone I speak to that Mr. Frank Ol is the man to see about the rental of South Tug, a village inhabited mostly by second- and third-generation Polish Americans. Michel Bontemps walks along the main street. To his astonishment he is not recognized despite the large spread about him in the local papers. Wearing a blue shirt and sandals Bontemps is walking along Main Street, tasting as well as testing the surfaceness of all American things. The sidewalk is American, the buildings are American, the faces are authentic American with traces of the bark that centuries ago peeled off the thick impenetrable forests in Poland. This is America, he exultantly tells Jill. Feel it, feel it . . . doesn't the surface feel different . . .

Michel Bontemps is a difficult man to describe, I inform the Mayor of the town. Bontemps has survived a dozen close friendships, a dozen accidents, a dozen apartments in different locations, a dozen film festivals. Is he still a Marxist, asks the Mayor. He uses a great deal of color on the screen, I reply cautiously. Aesthetically he is quite pure, if you follow what I mean. Unfortunately, I have some difficulty with my eyesight, says the Mayor. I rarely go to the movies, I never even watch the reruns on TV. We are to visit the Mayor tomorrow. When can we meet the architect of your incredible Utopian Mall, I asked the Mayor as I was leaving. Oh, Ite . . . I'm afraid that's impossible. He's been missing for three years.

4

This is a familiar world. It is crowded with familiar faces. Mr. Cas Ite's face was just such a face until he disappeared. The large windowless structure he designed fitted in nicely with the needs of the two adjacent communities. Thanks to the Mall, their needs can now be met more efficiently and economically. Michel feels downcast. He has with my assistance counted on interviewing the architect of the Mall. An impromptu interview with nothing deleted . . . close-up of Ite's intense face, Ite's hands, Ite smoking, Ite coughing, Ite hesitating, at a loss for a word, Ite receiving a telephone call, Ite speaking in a colorless voice . . . But Mr. Cas Ite disappeared in June three years ago. He left just after breakfast, explained Mrs. Ite. He was going out for a pack of cigarettes, in other words, for a most common and reasonable need. He never returned. In the past he had never been in the habit of telling her that he was leaving the house. He did not keep her informed as to his movements. His explanation that morning was an exception, but at that time she didn't notice it. She didn't even look up when he left the room. She also didn't clearly recall what he was wearing. She was immersed in drawing up a list of names for their annual garden party.

As usual, a number of names that had been on the list the year before were deleted. Mr. Merce Ite, Cas Ite's brother, was conspicuously absent from the list for the fourth or fifth time. When Mr. Ite left the room on his way to buy a pack of cigarettes he slammed the door. The brain is terribly selective. Mrs. Ite remembers Mr. Ite forcefully slamming the door, but for the life of her, she can't recall why he did so. He has now been missing for three years, and his disappearance has become to all utterly and totally familiar. Everyone in town remembers him, and instantly is able to remember the few and sparse details of his disappearance. It was Mr. Ite who over a period of years shaped the town's needs by replacing many of the familiar landmarks with structures that have since become equally familiar. By now, no one can recall the cornfield upon which the Mall was built.

5

It's a great pity about Ite, said Michel Bontemps. I had hoped he'd clarify the materialistic concerns that are the basis of his Utopian vision. Are the three of you living together, I am unexpectedly asked by the desk clerk at the hotel where we are staying. We have come to America, I patiently explain, to make a film exploring America's needs. The Mall on Route 11 exemplifies those needs. Our own sexual needs, I am convinced, are no different from your own. They are, to some degree, determined by the topography of our interior space, and by the availability and accessibility of an acquiescent sexual partner. It so happens that the three of us are simply friends working on a film. We happen to share a double bed, but why focus on that. We also share our food and items of clothing, as well as our money.

That afternoon for the first time we visited the Mall. It was a tremendous disappointment visually. We had expected it to be larger, more monstrous and ugly. To our dismay we found that it blended in nicely with the American landscape, and its inoffensiveness troubled us. Is this what had brought us here? To get to the Mall we had to take a taxi. I sat next to the driver, while Jill and Michel sat in the back. As far as I can determine, this was not a preconceived plan on their part. I hardly gave it a thought. The taxi driver casually mentioned that someone in this community had a few years ago named their child Bontemps. We were all terribly amused. The brain is incredibly selective, and quick to dismiss certain items of information. One has next to no control over this process of selection. Michel wore the blue shirt he had worn on the previous day. All I seem to remember of the afternoon is the half hour I spent by myself playing a pinball machine in the Mall. I had invited Jill and Michel to join me, but they wanted to walk around and explore the stores instead.

Why don't you visit Mr. Frank Ol to see if he'll let us rent the village and the equipment we need, said Michel on our return from the Mall. The hotel room is our center, our HQ . . . our books, our papers, our black-and-white photographs of Che and Mao have diminished the bleak plastic uniformity of the surfaces in our room. We have, for the duration of our presence, imposed on the neutral hotel surface the dynamics of our ideas and intentions.

6

This is my son, Bud, said Mrs. Ite. She sees him daily. She sees him the way she sees everything that is terribly familiar. She sees him slouching on an armchair that has recently been upholstered, she sees him driven by predictable needs, needs that the stores on Main Street are able to satisfy for the time being. One day he will inherit a share of the Mall, and his needs may change . . . He is attached to me, she explains. Naturally, he is also attached to his car, to his friends, and to this house which his father designed. It is a large spacious building with two rather massive white columns framing the entrance. Most of the furniture has also been designed by Mr. Ite, and so has the elaborate labyrinthlike pattern on the rug in the living room. The rug was woven on a special loom in Turkey. Bud Ite is standing on it. His large feet are planted on the somewhat faded design. The carpet simply provides a surface for his feet. He has just returned from Mr. Ol's office on Main Street. Mr. Ol has this afternoon revealed to Bud some of the intricacies of the real estate business. Mr. Ol has, furthermore, with great fanfare, given Bud a desk in an office adjacent to his own. It is an exhilarating beginning. The old scarred green metal desk has four drawers on the left side. It is entirely up to Bud how he wishes to arrange his papers. No one will interfere, no one will pry. In addition to the desk, there's a swivel chair, and a two-drawer filing cabinet, and, he has been promised, the partial or part-time use of a secretary whose name is Witty. Witty is divorced and thirty-eight. She smiled at Bud and took him on a tour of the office. She is a young-looking thirty-eight Bud decided. This is your office, she said. This is your desk, and this is your swivel chair, just don't lean back too far. Ha ha. This is the john, and this is where we hang the key to the john. This is my office, and over here, next to yours, is Mr. Ol's. Bud was also introduced to half a dozen other clerks and messenger boys. He also met Sloan, the man who ran the elevator. It is, he was told, the oldest elevator in town. Consequently the man running it is well known. A number of American Presidents have made use of the elevator during the last one hundred years. A number of them have met and been introduced to Sloan. Before leaving he was handed the keys to the office. He attached them to his key chain. He now had a total of six keys, two for his car, which he drives with a certain practiced abandon. Eager to tell Mrs. Ite about his afternoon at Frank Ol's office, he hurriedly parked the car, and walked to the house. The front door was locked. He pulled out his key chain that was now heavier by two keys. Ever since he had moved into another room on the first floor he was able to exclude the second from his mind. In the past, going to his room had entailed climbing the stairs. Although his brain now excluded the second floor, he would sometime head for the stairs, and be half way up, before he remembered where he was staying. Entering the house, he could hear Mrs. Ite laughing. She was entertaining someone. She had a pleasant laugh. It was, in some respects, a difficult laugh to fathom since technically she was still married, or at any rate, not divorced. The laugh of a divorced woman is frequently interpreted by a man to signify some future if as yet unspecified need. Bud Ite is only twenty-four, and the uncertainty of his needs are colliding in his brain. When, for instance, Mr. Ol's secretary laughed he was instantly made aware of the insecurity of her needs. Mrs. Ite laughed at something I said. It was something intentionally flattering in order to provoke the laugh. Furthermore I spoke with a distinct French accent, an advantage in this case. She was not familiar with Bontemps but listened attentively when I mentioned his great desire to film the Mall. I had already spoken to Mr. Ol, and the Mayor, and Mr. Bilb, the trial lawyer and silent partner of Mr. Ite and Mr. Ol. It was at their suggestion that I was having tea with Mrs. Ite . . . I mentioned Michel Bontemps's reputation as an innovative filmmaker in Europe. Aren't the three of you staying together in one hotel room, she asked, all the while staring at me. Not any longer, I was able to reply. You see, Michel Bontemps and Jill have had to return to Paris, leaving me behind to make all the necessary arrangements. Once those are complete, Bontemps will return with a film crew. Mrs. Ite and I are seated only four or five feet apart in the living room. She now crosses her legs. I interpret it as a deliberate act. They are attractive legs. They are the essential accoutrement for so many needs. She is just as familiar as I with these needs. She demonstrates the agility with which a need can dominate the brain to the exclusion of other needs, by exposing her legs to my view. I promptly said yes, when she asked me if I was free for dinner.

7

When Bontemps left he took my Gillette razor and thirty-five Seconals I kept in the cabinet at the side of the bed. He left abruptly because he had no desire to confront me face to face. Instead he left a hand-written note, stating somewhat bluntly: I have fucked Jill. I'm sure that my saying I did not intend to does not alter the fact, or the pain this might cause you. I know we had agreed not to permit sex to interfere with our joint project. I do not wish to hide from you that I feel quite miserable about this, having known that you two planned to get married as soon as the film was completed. As I now leave, I reproach myself for not staying. . . . Despite what has happened I should stay, and under any other circumstance, I would do so, but I must also, I regret to say, admit to a feeling of distrust and growing antipathy toward you. It is only a matter of time before you will start to write, as have all the others, and exploit my ideas. I have no particular desire to take Jill with me. I urged her to remain behind, but she insisted on leaving to spare you the embarrassment you would doubtlessly feel were she to remain. I must add that I had no intention whatever of screwing Jill. For one thing, she's not my type. Physically she does not appeal to me. It was, you may be interested to know, one of the reasons I so readily agreed to have you both work as my assistants. The letter was signed, Bontemps. It was a typical letter from Bontemps. I counted at least seventeen personal pronouns. I read it carefully, committing the contents to memory, then I destroyed the letter, and promptly forgot the gist of it. The mind is so terribly selective. I would just as soon not have my memory jogged into awareness by letters that have been left lying around.

8

This is my story. Without Bontemps it wouldn't have been possible. Thank you, Michel Bontemps.

9

This is a familiar world. I do not object to the familiar. On the contrary, I welcome it. I lie awake at night thinking of Jill and Bontemps. Tomorrow Bud Ite will take me on a tour of the Mall. He is extremely excited at the thought of working with me on the film, and meeting Bontemps and Jill once they return. But I've never acted before, he said. That's perfectly all right, Bontemps prefers to work with people who have had no prior acting experience, I assured him. All you will have to do, when on camera, is to think of your needs. Bud looked at me, alarmed, asking: What are my needs?

Bud is Mr. Ite's only son. He shares the ground floor of the building with his mother. Although their bedrooms, I've been able to determine, are quite far apart, he can now hear his mother's laugh more frequently than ever before. She does not inquire what he does with his time. She does not visit his room. It doesn't matter. Like her Bud knows every inch of the house his father designed. Each year Bud would mingle among the guests at the garden party. He would greet them by name whenever possible. He would answer their questions. The garden party, the faces, the questions were familiar. He felt as if he had lived with them all his life. He wasn't particularly proud that his father had designed this house and the furniture in it, and stipulated where everything should be placed, as well as selecting the color of the curtains and carpets. To Bud it was just another house, and the newly built Mall was just another Mall. The day Mr. Ite left the house he slammed the door of the room in which his wife happened to be sitting. He did not take one of the cars, or call for a taxi. Naturally, after his disappearance the garden party was canceled. Mr. Frank Ol came by soon after the disappearance. At his advice Mrs. Ite had the house painted. It was in need of a fresh coat of paint. It cheered her up considerably.

PART TWO

1

Frank Ol is a large man. He likes to be comfortable. He likes large comfortable leather armchairs. When he leaves the office he can either go home or visit Mrs. Ite. Sometimes he does one, sometimes the other. He prefers the Ite house largely because it is cooler and more comfortable. He sits in an armchair that has been purchased since the disappearance of Mr. Ite and reads the paper. Across from him sits Mrs. Ite. She respects his incredible drive and energy. She also respects his cunning. Frank Ol, unlike her husband, is totally unpredictable. She sits across from Mr. Ol, her lovely legs crossed, waiting for him to lower the newspaper.

Mr. Ol now has a key to the front door. The key is on his key chain, and each time he pulls it out at the office or at home he is shamelessly exposing the new attachment for everyone to see. With the exception of the study upstairs, all the other rooms are open. One does not need a key to enter any particular room . . . Mr. Ol enters one room and then another . . . Fascinated she watches as he arranges the furniture, and thereby channels the topography of his need, while, at night, Bud tosses sleeplessly on his bed. He is familiarizing himself with the sound of heavy footsteps, and with the other sometimes prolonged unfamiliar sounds . . . He has known Mr. Ol ever since he was a young boy. Frank Ol, Mr. Bilb the trial lawyer, the town Mayor, and his father used to play poker once a week in Mr. Ol's office. Quite frequently Mr. Ite and the others would prefer to return home by taxi. Mr. Ite would call the Chivalry Cab Co. on Main Street. Geraldine, the taxi dispatcher, remembers him well. Mostly she remembers his soft and pleasant voice. He would always ask after her husband Hank. How's Hank today, he would ask, although it was two in the morning. She, in turn, would try to sound lighthearted and gay. She would say: Oh, Hank, why he's just dandy . . . He's now on the day shift at the plant. Why, we hardly see each other . . .

This is an introduction to the 7-Up bottling plant. The Mayor cut the red ribbon at the plant's opening ceremony. His secretary Clara had to guide his hand, because he couldn't see the ribbon. The forklifts and the trucks were neatly lined up on the huge cement parking lot to the left of the two buildings that had been designed by Mr. Ite. After only two days Hank found the work a trifle monotonous. He drove a forklift and kept moving huge crates of 7-Up. During the lunch hour he and his new buddies would play a game of softball on the parking lot. No one objects. No one cares what the men do with their own time. No one seems to mind that they are using up the surface of the parking lot. No one in the front office at the bottling plant shows any interest in what the men have to say to each other, and no one minds that they take the dented cans, many dented deliberately, home to their wives and kids. It has become the custom and is by now a familiar pattern. The Mayor in an interview on local TV asserts that the bottling plant will make the town prosperous again. But it is hard to prove. He also, in a later interview, claimed that the new Mall would put the town on the map by attracting outside capital. But so far, all it did was to draw away some of the customers from Main Street. Geraldine prefers the Mall, and so does Hank. They prefer the newness of the surfaces that cover the floors and walls, they prefer the music, the fountain, the pinball machines, the oneness of it all. A pleasant sensation as the past is displaced by the activity of the indoor fountain, the five movie houses, the two restaurants, the forty-five stores. There is also ample parking. Geraldine often wonders where Mrs. Ite does her shopping. And where does the young and pretty wife of the Mayor do her shopping . . . she has never seen either of them at the Mall.

3

This is an introduction to Hank's eye. Their apartment is on the third floor. All the buildings in the immediate vicinity are alike. They were built and designed by Mr. Ite shortly before he disappeared. With the assistance of Mr. Ol, Hank and Geraldine were able to get a four-room apartment at a time when apartments in these buildings were in great demand, as they still are. Geraldine chose the furniture. The bedroom is all in black and white. A white shag rug, white furniture, white drapes, a black dressing table with a large oval mirror, a black built-in closet, a black headboard for the double bed. They each have their possessions . . . Hank is forever surprised by the things he finds in their apartment. He has no recollection of ever having bought most of the things that are lying about. His three suits hang in the closet, next to at least two dozen dresses he does not recognize.

Sunday he reads the *Gazette*. Sunday he has a quiet beer on the balcony. Sunday he does not see his buddies. When he enters the bedroom he feels that he is entering someone else's bedroom. He feels that he is trespassing. He enters and finds Geraldine examining her body in front of the mirror. It is, needless to say, a familiar body to her. It is showing signs of age. Almost daily she familiarizes herself with herself and with every inch of her body, evaluating it, inch by inch. The black bra and panties she is wearing help her make a general assessment of her appeal to men . . . She is now seeing herself as others must have seen her. This is what they saw, she says to herself. This is what they are missing. She is not oblivious of Hank's presence. He is something that came over from the old apartment. I'll never tell you anything about the men in my life, she says. The room is air conditioned. Hank usually falls asleep the moment his head hits the pillow. On Sunday he insists on reading to her every article in the local paper that refers to the Mayor, or Mr. Ol, or Mrs. Ite, the wife of the missing architect. He also reads to her a description of Michel Bontemps. That's funny, he says. You named Bontemps after this guy, didn't you. She can sense that he is proud of her. Proud of her achievements, of her capabilities, of her choice of the furniture, and this apartment. When he sees her dressed only in her bra and panties, examining herself in the mirror, he sits back in the new bucketlike plastic chair, his feet resting on the white shag rug, a look of satisfaction on his face. Do you want to make love, he asks. Not now, she answers, I'm busy, can't you see.

4

Everyone knows that Mr. Ite is missing, and there are all kinds of conflicting stories about his sudden and inexplicable disappearance.

One story has it that Mr. Ite is the father of Geraldine's son, Bontemps . . . and that Hank, when he found out, killed Mr. Ite. But Hank, as everyone well knows, is incapable of such an action. He is much too inept, and much too much in awe of Mr. Ite. Others claim that Hank is not inept at all. After all, long before Mr. Ite's disappearance, Hank had been the local table tennis champion. No one had expected him to win the championship at the time. Mr. Ite, Mr. Ol, Mr. Bilb, and the Mayor had attended the final match of the championship which took place at the local Y. Geraldine remembers the evening quite clearly. That one occasion when she had no regrets whatever at having married Hank. Hank had demonstrated to everyone that he was capable of being the town's table tennis champion. Mr. Ite and his friends and partners, Mr. Ol, Mr. Bilb, and the Mayor, had all greeted her warmly. She noticed that they all had come without their wives. They kept smiling and looking at her fixedly, remembering who she was, saying: you're an awfully lucky girl. Hank is a terrific player and a terrific guy. Yes, they all had the most vivid memories of their past encounter with her. They remembered her name. They were busy and successful men with a great deal on their minds, yet they remembered certain almost inconsequential and trite details. They recalled what they had said to her, and what she had replied. They were able to remember the surfaces of couches, leather armchairs, the carpeted floor, and smooth white table tops. By stretching their memories, their elastic memories, they were able to bring to life the interiors in which they had first seen Geraldine in black bra and panties . . . The brain is highly selective, and also at times highly unreliable. They had been celebrating the decision to build the Mall. Mr. Ol had arrived with Geraldine. She was wearing a sleeveless pink dress. Mr. Ol introduced her to the others, explaining to her the nature of the celebration. Celebrations are quite commonplace. Sometimes the most trivial events are celebrated. In this instance it was the Mall. Mr. Ol had explained the reason for the celebration without being the least bit condescending. He spoke to her the way he would have spoken to anyone else. She understood the significance of the event, as well as the rewards the four men anticipated . . . celebrations, too, can be rewarding. One time, she, Geraldine, had been regarded as a reward. She rewarded them . . . and was, in turn, rewarded . . .

By winning the championship Hank had put these powerful men

in a good humor, and they rewarded him with applause, and on the following day offered him a job at the bottling plant, even though the bottling plant was still in the planning stages at the office of Mr. Ite. For six full months Hank had been able to collect a salary without putting in a stroke of work. He didn't ask any questions. He was content. Now that people on the street recognized him and bought him drinks he was content. The future seemed brighter. But soon after their first child was born he stopped going out. He remained glued to the TV set in the living room until the bottling plant opened.

Once during her pregnancy Geraldine had gone by herself to see a foreign film. It was a film by Michel Bontemps. In the film the principal character was driving a car containing two kilos of hash from Antwerp. Stopped for speeding by a policeman, a familiar quandary, he shot the policeman. A few days later, back in Antwerp, he runs into a young American woman, and having determined that she is sexually available, sleeps with her. In bed they speak about a great many irrelevant things. Some of the irrelevant things he keeps repeating intrigue her and amuse her. It is his way of forming an attachment. He has just killed a cop, yet he permits himself to be distracted by her, and postpones his departure. Geraldine was struck by his diffidence, his emotional lethargy, and his need for the woman, a need he keeps trying to disguise. Toward the end of the film the young American woman in a gratuitous gesture turns him in to the police. He makes a half-hearted attempt to escape and is killed. For some reason she could not quite understand, Geraldine could see herself making a similar call to the police, turning in a couple of men. She strongly identified herself with the woman. Anyone who has seen the film is well aware that Bontemps did not identify himself with the woman. He identified himself with the hunted man who is shot at the wheel of his car with the motor running. Geraldine did not mention her reactions to the film to Hank, since he would not have understood. Neither did she tell him that on a moment's impulse she had written a letter to Bontemps. Not having the filmmaker's address she sent the letter to the French Embassy in Washington. Two years later she received a reply. Dear Geraldine, thank you for thinking of me. I'm glad you liked the film. I do too. And it was signed, Michel Bontemps. The only person who ever saw the letter was Mr. Merce Ite, Cas Ite's brother. She showed it to Merce because he frequently went to Boston to see a play, and because he was known to read books. However, despite his knowledge of the arts, he was not familiar with Bontemps. But he said he was glad for her. Geraldine knew he meant it. Poor, poor Merce, always excluded by the others. He had never slept with her. How do you feel having a successful brother, she once asked.

5

Mr. Merce Ite does not speak to Sloan the elevator operator, and in turn, Sloan does not speak to him. Merce passes Sloan at least four times a day and frequently as much as a dozen times a day, but by now they no longer even see each other. The elevator operator sits on a little plastic-covered seat inside the tiny elevator cage, or, on a nice day, leans against the doorframe of the entrance to the building. Mr. Merce Ite does not any longer count the number of times he passes Sloan daily, but he does count the number of times he runs into Mr. Ol, and the number of times he runs into Mr. Ol's secretary. There are other people in the building beside these two, but for Merce, each encounter with Mr. Ol and with his secretary are of an overriding importance. For one thing, Mr. Ol was a close friend and business associate of his missing brother, for another, Mr. Ol also happens to own the building, and this has enabled him to deny Mr. Merce Ite the use of the elevator . . . Mr. Ol claimed that Mr. Merce Ite was misusing the elevator . . . that he was constantly going up or down simply in order to engage Sloan in a lengthy conversation . . . this in turn distracted Sloan. Witty, Mr. Ol's secretary, is privy to everything Mr. Ol does. Once, at Christmas, Mr. Merce Ite had given her a bouquet of roses. Once, Mr. Merce Ite had been on friendly terms with Sloan. They had daily exchanged how do you do's, and small snippets of conversation. After Mr. Ol had told Merce not to use the elevator, communication with Sloan became strained. After all, Merce reasoned, Sloan was an employee of Mr. Ol, yet no one had told Sloan not to speak to Mr. Merce Ite, or not to respond to Merce's cordial greeting. Still, the strain was very visible. It inhibited their greetings and their exchanges regarding the weather. Finally, one day Mr. Merce Ite passed Sloan without greeting him. It was not an easy thing to do. At first, the following week, when Merce passed Sloan, both men would grit their teeth to hold back the familiar "hi" that might involuntarily pass their lips. If Mr. Ol was pleased by what had happened, he gave no sign of it. In general, Mr. Ol considered Merce a nuisance, someone he wanted out of the building. Not letting Merce use the elevator was simply one way of compelling Merce to leave the building. Mr. Ol spent a good deal of his spare time thinking up ways of annoying Merce Ite. Occasionally, however, Mr. Ol was busy with his own affairs. It's one of those days, Witty would say to Mr. Merce Ite as she passed his office. Unlike Sloan, who was, after all, only the elevator operator, Witty had never stopped speaking to Mr. Merce Ite . . . Perhaps she had never forgotten his bouquet of roses.

Mr. Merce Ite is always busy. His brain is forever alert for the changes, the imperceptible changes that take place daily. He records those changes in order better to understand the familiar world around him. A long time ago, when he first moved into his office, Mr. Merce Ite had a telephone installed. The telephone is still in the same place on his desk, but it seldom rings. In fact, Merce cannot recall the last time he heard it ring. Still, the telephone is a useful instrument, and he makes good use of it. Daily he calls the airport, the two local newspapers, the weather information, the public library, the army and navy recruitment office, the Mayor's office, the Department of Public Works. Invariably he first dials 411 for information, then dials the number he received from information, explaining his need to whoever answers the phone. His needs, in most instances, are simple, direct, forthright, and immediately taken care of. He is promptly given the correct time, the weather forecast for the next six hours, the title and author of a certain book, the correct spelling of the Chief of Staff, etc. On the phone, Mr. Merce Ite speaks with a measured sense of his own dignity. When not on the phone, he solves crossword puzzles. A month after his brother had disappeared, Mr. Merce Ite was notified by Mr. Ol not to use the toilet on the second floor. Since Witty refused to deliver the message to Merce, Mr. Ol himself slipped a memo under Merce's door during one of the latter's infrequent absences from his office. The memo was couched in the appropriate office jargon. It simply stated that according to a number of reliable witnesses, Mr. Merce Ite, whenever he used the urinal in the toilet, failed to direct the stream of his urine at the urinal, and then, having soiled the floor, used wads of toilet paper to wipe his hands, perfunctorily dropping the paper on the floor instead of discarding it in the container that had at great expense been provided by the management for that very purpose. The use of the toilet was a privilege that could be revoked if the person in question ignored the fundamental rules of hygiene. The memo concluded by stating that Mr. Merce Ite, if he so wished, could use the toilet in the bar on the street level. Merce took the memo in his stride. It was not very often that anyone sent him a memo. He read it carefully. He didn't make a fuss, he didn't loudly accuse Mr. Ol of being a fucking son of a bitch. He simply methodically reduced the intake of liquids. Life goes on. Each day, in *The New York Times,* a crossword puzzle challenges the brain. The word "urine," Merce noticed, is never used. It is a five-letter word listed in the dictionary between urinate and uriniferous tubule. Yet, it is as if the designer of the puzzle has permanently excluded the five-letter word from the solutions toward which Merce's brain is forever reaching.

6

Geraldine sits at her desk in a small room that is situated directly above the CLEAVO dry cleaners. The walls in the room could do with a coat of paint, but Geraldine is reluctant to ask the owners to have it done. She is reluctant to ask anything for herself. From where she sits she has an unencumbered view of the opposite side of Main Street. Looking to the right she can see a section of the Town Hall. Sometimes she catches a glimpse of the busy Mayor as he leaves the Town Hall. She recognizes his face, even at that distance. On a few precious prior occasions she has seen his face from extremely close up, only inches away, until his face moving even closer, removed all distance between them. Yet despite the former proximity of their faces, she has never been to the Mayor's house. Now, whenever they meet, he greets her politely. The greeting is somewhat lacking in warmth, but it is polite. He has never introduced her to his wife. If she had played her cards right she could now be the Mayor's wife. That's what her parents had said when she gave birth to Bontemps. That's what her best friend, Eilene, also had said. Instead she married Hank. At that time he was a promising table tennis player at the Y. The Mayor, Mr. Ol, Mr. Ite, and Mr. Bilb were on the board of trustees at the Y. Naturally, they were pleased by Hank's achievement. The four men also owned the bottling company, the taxi company, the new Mall, and a dozen other enterprises. After the bottling plant opened Hank would each day bring home a six-pack of 7-Up. For the first time since he had won the table tennis championship, Hank seemed truly happy. He was working together with a nice bunch of guys. He enjoyed the daily ballgames on the parking lot. He never visited the Y although Geraldine kept urging him to.

The Ites live in the vicinity of the Y where Hank had received the gold trophy from the Mayor. Driving past the Ite house, Geraldine saw both cars in the driveway, and a gardener clipping the hedges. One day she had caught sight of the Mayor and his wife leaving the Ite place. To her surprise, when the Mayor and his wife passed her, he pretended not to recognize her. He probably did not see you, Hank said afterward.

7

This is an introduction to the Mayor's bad eyesight. Of late he can hardly make out his own shoes. He hesitates before approaching his desk for fear that he might find someone else seated behind it, something that Mr. Ol had once threatened to do to him. The Mayor avoids whenever possible all public meetings. He also avoids the bottling plant, and dreads the weekly poker games. At night, exhausted, he falls into bed, not seeing his attractive wife lying naked at his side. At least, he has confided to his wife, ever since Cas Ite has disappeared we no longer need go to those awful garden parties. I don't recognize anyone, and I can't recall their names when I do. There's a woman, I believe, who keeps waving to me from a window above the dry cleaners on Main Street every time I leave my office. What should I do?

The Mayor's polished black shoes are placed at the foot of his bed each night. Without his glasses his wife is daily beginning more and more to resemble a woman called Geraldine he once met at a small party organized by Ol. Ol had a talent for organizing parties. As he lies exhausted on the bed, the Mayor sees an undressed woman moving restlessly about the room. The naked woman keeps asking him what he did the entire day. She remembers everything he tells her. She has an unusual retentive and photographic memory. Are you still infatuated with that slut, she asks. He recoils in horror. Geraldine? How can I possibly be infatuated with a woman who has been screwed by every man in this town.

Geraldine locks the door and undresses. She remembers the Mayor's black shoes. On one occasion she remembers untying the laces, and then guiding his hand, saying, here, this is what you must have been looking for. Yes, he had sighed. It was everything he had dreamt it would be. It was everything Ol had promised it would be. But he was not yet the Mayor. He was simply one of Ol's lackeys. One day you will be the Mayor of this town, Geraldine had said, and he had made love to her with a renewed vigor.

8

After his father had disappeared Bud sat on his bed staring at the flatness of the world in front of his eyes. He wore a white polo shirt and white pants. The unfamiliar when it occurs changes, momentarily, the needs the familiar is able to provide. Bud drives a car, knifing through the familiar with the unerring unseeing ease of a born driver. One day he called for a taxi . . . he sounded almost incoherent on the phone. It was the day his father had disappeared. Is anything the matter, asked Geraldine. Can I help? She recognized his voice, just as he recognized hers. It was a warm June night, but despite the heat the Mayor wore his suit and tie. He was working late. He was afraid of his naked wife. Hand me my pen, he said to Clara, his secretary. Hand me my diary, I would like to make an entry. He wrote: Just heard from Frank. Cas Ite has disappeared. After some hesitation he added the letters WAR. They stood for, What a relief.

A few days later the police paid him a brief visit. They also visited Mr. Ol, Mr. Bilb, and Geraldine. They treated her with far less respect than they had the others. They asked her if she had screwed around with Mr. Ite . . . and if it was true that Ite was a son of a bitch who thought that he was a cut above the others. She stared at them, not at all intimidated, not at all frightened. What else would you like to know, she asked. Would you also like to know if I've been screwed by the Mayor and Mr. Frank Ol and Mr. Bilb the trial lawyer. The two men who came to the taxi office suddenly discovered that their relaxed faces had grown heavy . . . and that their jaws were suffering from a muscular fatigue. Later in the day they made their report. They said that when they entered the Mayor's office he had stared blankly at them. They were simply two silhouettes against a familiar flatness on which were hung a couple of photographs of the Mayor and his buddies, Ite, Ol, and Bilb. The officers had addressed him as: Mr. Mayor and Sir. Sometimes one, sometimes the other. He answered their questions, explaining that he had seen Cas Ite the day before his disappearance. They had discussed a new civic center that Mr. Ite was eager to design. The center would have ample parking, and would help rejuvenate the town, spiritually as well as culturally.

Several months later Geraldine ran into the Mayor. On this occasion he was alone. He recognized her and even remembered her name. He greeted her warmly, and then, with a flushed face and a look of elation told her that he and his wife would be moving into a new house, and that they had just purchased eight thousand dollars' worth of modern furniture. His wife, he admitted, preferred the modern to the traditional, but he had begun to adjust himself to it. From his face she could see that he didn't really mind. She did not refer to her son Bontemps, and neither did he. Each month, in addition to her salary she receives a check for one hundred and fifty dollars from Mr. Ol's office. The check comes in a plain white envelope. If Hank is aware of this additional source of income he is tactful enough not to inquire. He lets her open all the mail for fear that he might inadvertently open the wrong envelope. She deposits fifty in a savings account and uses the remainder for living expenses. The money has enabled them to move into a larger and more modern apartment. The apartment came with a dishwasher, air conditioning, wall-to-wall carpeting, washing machine and dryer. Twice a year they drive to Pittsfield and visit Bontemps. He is six years old. They are teaching him to put on his own clothes, they are also teaching him to wash his face and hands in the morning and before bedtime. He is having some trouble putting on his shoes, but Geraldine is reassured by the man in charge of the program that this is not unusual. There are five retarded boys and seven retarded girls in Bontemps's class, but Bontemps is the only one among the group who also happens to be blind. He seems happy enough whenever they see him. He solemnly sits on Hank's bony knees and listens to Hank explain how table tennis is to be played. Both Geraldine and Hank are convinced that Bontemps, despite their prolonged absence, continues to recognize them . . . they fondly recall how he had clutched their hands as they had toured the grounds of the institution. They use special words that will enable Bontemps to understand what they are saying, or failing that, he will at least not feel excluded. Bibab, babib, babab bibub, says Hank, and Bontemps responds: Bibab, babib . . . He is a friendly little tyke, said Hank on their last visit. It was in some respect an unusual statement for Hank to make. Hank was unaccustomed to making statements or observations of any kind, no matter what the situation . . . At least he has a few friends now, said Geraldine. Yes, said Hank after a pause. I know exactly how he feels.

Of course, like the others, Mr. Cas Ite had known of Bontemps's existence. He also had known of the one hundred and fifty dollars Geraldine received each month. It stood to reason that he was informed, since it was he who had offered Geraldine the job as taxi dispatcher. The job is not a strenuous one . . . but it is a tedious one. She has lots of time on her hands. She spends a good deal of her time looking out of the window. In the far distance are the mountains, but unfortunately they are obscured by the three- and four-story buildings across the street. She still does not know why she decided to name her son Bontemps. It was done on an impulse. Everyone had objected because it was a foreign-sounding name, and because they had never heard of Michel Bontemps or seen any of his movies . . . but then, as soon as they learnt that the boy was blind and retarded they dropped their objections, and she had her way.

9

He will never see the world, he will never experience the pleasures we have experienced, Geraldine told her husband. He will never, as I had hoped, become the Mayor of this town. He will never even be the local table tennis champion. Everyone in town still remembers Hank's fantastic backhand smash, and his incredible serves. They still recall the unexpected ferocity with which he attacked and finally defeated the other player. For him it was an unexpected ferocity, perhaps fed in part by the presence of Ol and Ite and the Mayor. At that time and place he had for once fully understood what he was doing. He had comprehended how the white ping-pong ball would rebound from the hard green wood surface on the other half of the table. Hank had been filled with elation as he smashed the white ball into the right and into the left corner of his opponent's side. For a brief while, within the particular context of that game, he understood the surfaceness of all objects, he further understood that the table's surface enabled him to overcome his opponent strategically, and that consequently, given a different weapon, the surface of the wall, or floor, or office desk was just as well suited to an encounter between two or more individuals, an encounter requiring an identical quickness, alertness, and ambition to win. During his game, most of the floor space in the gymnasium had been occupied by metal folding chairs set up in long even rows on either side of the ping-pong table, and these chairs in turn had been occupied by a wildly cheering mob of people, many of whom he recognized, many of whom he would see on his daily walks through town, many of whom had on one or another occasion sold him something, not knowing at the time that in the near or distant future they would stand and cheer as he defeated his opponent. Given Mr. Cas Ite's preoccupation with the design of buildings, it stood to reason that he too understood the surfaceness of all things, continuously impressing on one surface another surface that was more to his liking. Only recently, where the Mall now stands there had been a field owned by a farmer. Hank had frequently passed the field in his car without an inkling of what was to take its place.

The surfaces in the interior of the warehouse where he drives a forklift are constantly being altered as stacks of cans are shifted about. The arrangement of these stacks is pretty much left to the discretion of Hank and his buddies. They decide where to place a fresh load of 7-Up. Sometimes, as the cases of 7-Up are unloaded, it is an instantaneous decision. The men look to Hank for advice. It is he who selects the area where they will play softball. When the plant first opened, the Mayor arrived to cut the ribbon, and then in front of all the assembled guests and workers he shook Hank's hand. Despite his poor eyesight, with some assistance from his indispensable secretary, he spotted Hank. He still warmly greets Hank whenever he sees him on the street. He calls him Champ. He says: Hi Champ, and Hank in turn, says, Hi there, Mr. Mayor. How's it going? When Geraldine informed Hank that Mr. Cas Ite was missing, had in fact disappeared, Hank immediately got into his car and drove over to the Ite house. There were several dozen people silently standing on the sidewalk across from the house, but otherwise everything looked normal. Both cars were in the driveway. They could hear the gardener on the far side mowing the lawn.

Mr. Ite, who had always been so absorbed by the challenge of each surface, had slipped away without leaving a trace. The surface on which Hank daily drove his forklift was linked by long and narrow surfaces called roads to other broad surfaces. The people in the office of the bottling plant referred to the long and narrow surfaces not as roads but as networks. If Hank is traveling on a network, he is unaware of it. Both he and Geraldine put in long hours. He receives time and a half. There are so many things he doesn't know about Geraldine, about Mr. Ite, about Mr. Ol, but he can imagine what those things are. His imagination runs rampant on the surface of past events that may or may not have taken place at the Wiggs Inn, and the Hamilton Hotel, and the Park Motel. Returning home after work, Hank likes to sit in the kitchen. There is a certain satisfaction to be derived from looking at the appliances. Everything is still gleaming new, and that newness spreads a temporary contentment over his face. Only months ago, all these appliances were in large cardboard containers, being lifted and shifted by a forklift from one surface to another. He had readily agreed with Geraldine that it was impossible to keep Bontemps . . . Bontemps would have marred and stained the perfect gloss of their surfaces . . . Hank sits in the kitchen, convinced that the kitchen of Mr. Ite, or of the Mayor, could not be superior to theirs. Certainly, kitchenwise, they were equal.

10

By disappearing Mr. Ite has affected the future surface stability of the entire region. According to Mr. Ite, the long Mall was intended to function as a kind of service tunnel for the new towns that eventually were to be built at either end. Now that Cas Ite has disappeared, will those two towns ever materialize?

At some point in time Mr. Frank Ol acquired the front door key to the Ite house. He carries the key on his key chain. He does not hide it. He comes to the house to hear Mrs. Ite's laughter. It is a delicate and more sophisticated laugh than say the laugh of his secretary . . . The key enables him to enter the house without first ringing the doorbell. It enables him to walk to Mrs. Ite's bedroom, if he so wishes, or to the kitchen, or to the living room. He has the run of the entire house. It is in the living room, on the large oval table, that he places the blueprints for the house, and first brings up the subject of dividing the second floor. Mrs. Ite would derive a substantial income from renting out an apartment upstairs. The apartment would be self-contained, possessing a separate entrance. She would never even have to encounter the person staying up-stairs. He would take care of all the construction. He could see the flicker of uncertainty in her eyes. When Mr. Ol entered the house late at night, Bud would turn over in his bed. His mother had told him that Frank Ol had a key . . . it made her feel safer, she had explained. Still Bud tossed about in his bed. A few days later Mr. Ol took Bud aside and showed him the blueprints. Bud was more receptive than his mother had been. Frank Ol smiled at Bud. Bud tried to resist the smile . . . he fought against the smile, but Frank was more experienced. Frank persisted and finally won. When Bud returned Mr. Ol's smile, Mr. Cas Ite was still missing, and also missing it had by now been determined was one plaid suit, one white shirt, lightly starched, one necktie, underwear, a pair of dark brown shoes, a monogrammed handkerchief, a wallet containing credit cards, driver's license, and over one hundred dollars in cash. Also missing was one checkbook and all his keys. One of the keys opened the front door. This knowledge may have alarmed Mrs. Ite. A month later the local locksmith changed the locks on the front and back door. Both Bud and Frank Ol received new keys. Occasionally Mrs. Ite can be seen at a local concert or a horse show in the company of Mr. Frank Ol. Her son still drives the large Buick given him by his father. He also is frequently seen in the company of Mr. Ol. In fact Bud now has a desk at Mr. Ol's real estate office although his duties remain somewhat undefined and vague. Bud was tremendously pleased when he was invited to join the poker game on Tuesday with Mr. Ol and the Mayor and Mr. Bilb the trial lawyer.

11

Witty, Mr. Ol's secretary, has been working for him for over twelve years. She has blonde hair, and she is the only one who does not knock before entering his office. Every month, without having to be reminded, she types out a check for Geraldine. Mr. Ol signs it. The envelope along with other envelopes is dropped in the mail-box outside the building when Witty leaves at five. In a sense she is performing this task after her work is finished for the day. Most of the time she knows what all the envelopes contain. She knows the amount of each check. She is utterly reliable. She

knows that on certain days Mr. Ol likes to dictate a long letter with
the door locked. She also knows the perfume Mrs. Ite uses . . . Bud
keeps asking himself: does Frank screw her or not? He had readily
sided with Frank Ol when the matter of dividing the house had
come up. The following day Bud had for the first time sat behind
Frank's desk during the latter's absence from the office. You can
use my desk anytime I'm out, Frank had told him. You can use it
now, I'll be gone for the rest of the day. Use my secretary too . . .

I think I'd like to dictate a letter, Bud Ite said hesitantly when
Witty stepped into the room. Would you like me to undress first,
she promptly asked.

Bud comprehended what followed, yet the flattening out of the
surfaces, and the compression of time in Witty's face exposed him
to the instantaneous transition of the present to the past. I'm in
the past, he thought, as he clung to Witty's perfume, and attempted to replicate, to the extent that the brain can reproduce, a
kind of segmented Witty, the knees, the thighs, the parted legs,
the hair, the open mouth, seen against the more stable and geo-
metric features of the room and furniture.

The black letters on the milk-white glass office doors designate
the form that is expected of whoever enters through the doors.
Witty had long ago mastered the form.

PART THREE

1

This is an introduction to Mr. Merce Ite, the brother of the successful architect who disappeared three years ago. Each day Mr. Merce
Ite, who doesn't own a car, walks to his office neither looking to
the left or to the right. He holds himself stiffly erect as he walks.
It is a noticeable and special walk. No one else in town walks like
him. By now it is also a familiar walk. I never see anyone on the
street, Mr. Merce Ite once said. I look straight ahead. If anyone
snubs him he is quite unaware of it. The way he walks, in fact,
precludes his being snubbed. Yet Merce is a friendly man, and will
gladly discuss his brother, his brother's wife, his interests in the
theater, whenever anyone comes to visit his office. Twice a year
before his brother disappeared, the latter used to send a young

man around to Merce's office to accompany Merce to Boston, where the two of them would take in a play or two, and Merce would do some shopping. Merce, for some reason, preferred to shop for his suits in Boston. His brother Cas Ite never sent the same young man around, and Merce would sometime complain because the new companion was not as interesting as the preceding one had been. Since his brother's disappearance Merce has not been to Boston. He has not bought a new suit or any other article of clothing in the past three years. He never enters any of the local stores unless he absolutely has to. On his way to the office, he only stops to buy *The New York Times*. He is the only one in the entire office building who reads the *Times*. It is, if anything, another point of difference. The differences add up. They are mostly minute and imperceptible, but over the years they tend to add up.

Mr. Merce Ite arrives at his office at eight and leaves around seven. By arriving early and leaving late he avoids the others. In particular he avoids Frank Ol, whose offices occupy the entire third floor, with the exception of the small office space Mr. Merce Ite occupies. The office has no windows. It was carved out of a much larger space. It is also the least desirable space on the entire floor. It is situated right across from the old-fashioned open cage-like elevator. That is how I met Mr. Merce Ite. I was getting off the elevator. Thinking that he was Mr. Ol, I entered his office and explained that I was an associate of Bontemps, the French film-maker who had come here to make a film of America's needs. Let me shake your hand, said Mr. Ite, standing up. We need more people like you in this town. I could at once see that he was fasci-nated by my description of our intentions, unfortunately he had a habit of interrupting me, of interjecting his own needs, keeping me in his office for several hours.

2

Gradually I am getting to know more and more people in the town. I am still staying at the hotel, but thinking of moving into a small apartment. Daily I drop by to see Mr. Frank Ol. He is becoming increasingly interested in having Bontemps shoot a film using the new Mall. I am astonished to learn that the Mall is not a success. The stores in the Mall are losing money, a few have already closed. No one knows why. Perhaps Mr. Cas Ite, if he were around, would have an explanation. Mr. Ol has none, but he doesn't seem unduly worried, he doesn't really care, he admitted, if the Mall goes down the drain. All the same, he does have a few solutions. It is just possible, he said, that a film, shot in and around the Mall might induce people, for whatever reason, to visit the Mall and shop there . . . He seems willing to go along with every one of Bontemp's plans. He refers to them as eccentricities. Yes, Bontemps can destroy a few houses in South Tug, as long as the people living in these houses have been given ample warning, he can also build a gigantic bonfire of merchandise on the parking lot, and he can even destroy a section of the Mall, and also stage an uprising . . . although, I can see that Mr. Ol is not quite clear what is meant by the word, and I, without Bontemp's guidance, cannot be more explicit.

I inform him that I am daily in touch with Bontemps, and that Bontemps is seriously thinking of returning to film the Mall in the fall, or failing that early next year. He looks at me skeptically. He is trying to determine how much of what I say is true. He is also trying to determine what my needs are . . . or rather what Bontemps's needs may be. I am quite prepared to discuss them. Bontemps's needs are not fame or even financial success, although that cannot entirely be ruled out. Bontemps's needs are strictly political and aesthetical. Bontemps wishes to destroy people like you in his films. Mr. Ol is all attention. Clearly I am appealing to his rationale. But Bontemps, I continue, subverts the destruction of his enemies by his aesthetic concerns. In other words, the placement, the color, the objects, the motions, the juxtaposition of faces all combine to diminish the revolutionary content. I could see that somewhere I had lost Mr. Ol's attention. In a sense, I found it very easy to get along with him.

Witty, his secretary, told me that Mr. Ol is married, and a devoted father, whose family was forever uppermost on his mind. Yes, I said, it stands to reason. Once they've built the new apartment in the Ite house, you might consider moving in, said Mr. Ol. Mrs. Ite and her son, Bud, are extremely fond of you. I said I would have to give it some thought.

3

Mr. Merce Ite is sharpening his pencil. The pencil sharpener is attached to the right side of his desk. It is an old-fashioned sharpener and requires the use of both hands. The sharpener dates back to Mr. Merce Ite's first day in business as a real estate agent. His brother Cas had encouraged him to start the business. Initially Merce moved into a much larger office, but bit by bit Frank Ol has been cutting into his space . . . When Merce Ite first started to try and sell dilapidated old farms and abandoned garages that no one seemed to want, Frank Ol was still an assistant to his father. Now Frank Ol runs the town. Now he runs the near blind Mayor, and everything else, including the firm of architects that had previously been Mr. Cas Ite's firm. Since Mr. Cas Ite's disappearance, Mr. Ol no longer greets Merce Ite. But Ite is a patient man. This is demonstrated by the way he sharpens his pencil. The puzzle in *The New York Times* is only one of the many challenges he will have to face that day. By now, after years of solving the daily puzzle in the *Times,* he has come to realize that the challenges that confront him are in many respects similar to the challenge posed by the puzzle. They too require the correct word, the correct interpretation, the correct solution. As for his needs, they are remarkably simple . . . they are also being taken care of . . . his rent is being paid by his brother, and since the latter disappeared, it is, without his having said anything to anyone, being paid by Mrs. Ite . . . His wardrobe, it is true, has suffered greatly since his brother's disappearance, and so have his periodic cultural trips to Boston to take in a play or two. He misses the young men his brother would send over to escort him . . . he misses the overnight stay in a hotel in Boston . . .

Each day Mr. Merce Ite sharpens his pencil. He is in fact sharpening his wits. That's why he can remain unperturbed by the insults that are daily hurled at him. Yes, he told me, daily, I am the target of their insults . . . that's why he can remain calm and diffident when Frank Ol, the son of a bitch, complains to Witty only a few feet from his office, that Merce is keeping the door of his office open to spy on him . . . When Merce has sharpened his pencil to his satisfaction, he will concentrate on the first word, four letters, across, for village.

This is a familiar world. Thanks to language, thanks to maps, thanks to a few signs on the road, the brain can digest the surfaces of the areas that lie just beyond the familiar. In that way the familiar is expanded, is stretched, letter by letter, as Mr. Merce Ite, pencil in hand, fills in the missing words.

Occasionally the familiar landscape is menaced by an inexplic-

able occurrence. The day before he disappeared Mr. Cas Ite
stepped out of the elevator. He was on his way to see Frank Ol. Mr.
Merce Ite hid behind his newspaper to spare his brother the embarrassment of pretending not to see him. But this time Cas Ite entered
Merce's office. It was a friendly visit. Merce did not feel threatened
by his brother. He did not, for once, feel the need to prove how
busy he was. He remained relaxed, and made no attempt to hide
the crossword puzzle on his desk. We're all trapped by our needs,
said Cas Ite. I just want you to know that I hope you'll come to
our next garden party. Before he left he also said that Frank Ol
was a bit impatient these days, but not to let that worry him. We
have a perfect partnership.

4

Mr. Merce Ite has a sign on his door. It reads REAL ESTATE.
The door is always open. Once or twice a week someone will
wander in, sit down, and listen to Merce for an hour before they
realize that somehow they've made a mistake. It is a mistake that
is never repeated. Mr. Merce Ite doesn't mind. He likes an occasional visitor. He'll talk about real estate property, politics, Mr.
Frank Ol, Boston suits, the theater, he'll talk about anything. He's
a born conversationalist. He never runs out of something to say.
His brain keeps renewing itself . . . he does take some satisfaction
that he still receives lists of buildings that are for sale. They pile
up. Churches, homes, factories, warehouses, some of the brochures
containing photographs of the property. Sometimes it may happen
that Merce is familiar with the property in question. Then, reading the description of the building, the dimensions of the lot, he
will, in his mind, people it with faces that long ago used to greet
him, used to come forward, smiling, shaking his hand. Over the
years this has changed. It was an imperceptible change at first.
He remained oblivious of it for some time, until one evening he
realized that he had nowhere to go in the town where he was
born . . . The daytime was a different matter. He had access to
the town hall, the public library, the two colleges in the vicinity,
the public toilet in the courthouse, and as a result he also had
access to the people who could be found inside these buildings.
  Once Merce had been on good terms with Frank. Frank had

called him Merce, and he had called Ol, Frank. Once or twice they had a drink together. Frank liked to talk about women, women in general and women in particular, and he also liked to make fun of Merce, but it was all quite harmless. Merce didn't object. Merce used to laugh a lot at what Frank said, until one evening he saw Frank together with his brother's wife. They, Frank Ol and Cas's wife, were coming out of a hotel in Boston. They may have just met, reasoned Merce. Merce was together with one of his young chaperons, as he used to refer to them. He had just bought a light-weight suit, paid for by his brother Cas of course. Frank pretended not to see him. Mr. Merce Ite never mentioned this to anyone. He didn't really like his brother's wife, but he admired her efficiency, her way of organizing the house. From that time on, whenever he visited his brother, he would stare at the interior, at the way the food was being served, as if searching for some flaw, some error, something that would confirm what he had seen . . . but all this is ancient history . . .

Mr. Merce Ite misses the young men who would be sent over by his brother, misses the excitement of traveling to Boston, the excitement of sitting in the twelfth row and waiting for the curtain to rise in a theater. On subsequent visits, although he frequently passed the same hotel, he never again saw Frank or his brother's wife. He never said a word to his brother. His brother was the most prominent architect in the area. He and Frank were partners. Frank provided a lot of the capital, but that is general knowledge. This is a small town. Mr. Merce Ite has also seen Hank a number of times. He has never spoken to him, but he knows that Hank was at one time the table tennis champion. He also knows that Geraldine works as a dispatcher for the cab company. One day after Frank Ol had left the office she stepped out of the elevator. She had to speak to Frank. Merce beckoned her to enter his office. They spent a few hours talking. Merce told her to avoid Frank Ol. He didn't know what to do when she burst into tears.

Mr. Merce Ite lives alone. Everything he does in the evening is carefully thought out. A minimum of time is spent on the necessities, the ablution, the cooking, the cleaning up, the laundry . . . Naturally Merce would spend an occasional evening at his brother's house, but he hadn't been there in some time. He had always been invited to the annual garden party, until unaccountably one year the invitation did not arrive. He was sure that it had been lost in the mail, and had waited, patiently waited until the last moment, keeping himself in a state of preparedness, his white shirt ironed, his dark suit pressed, his shoes shined, his hair combed . . . but he bore his brother no rancor . . . It was Frank Ol who was instrumental at his not being invited . . . It was Frank Ol . . .

A long time ago, whenever he used to visit his brother Cas, Cas would pour him a drink, and then would listen to Merce speak about his trips to Boston, and his friendship with Jack Kennedy . . .

Like the Mayor, like Ol and Bilb the trial lawyer, Merce Ite knew that Bontemps and Jill and I had come to film the Mall. He had never, he admitted, seen any of Bontemps's films . . . He was not much interested in the cinema. He preferred the theater. At night he was working on a drama. It was a play about his friendship with the former President Kennedy, when the President was still a young senator. Merce told me that he had met John Kennedy when he, Merce, was teaching at a night school in Boston. Kennedy had just been discharged from the navy, and thinking of his future, had gone to night school to take lessons in elocution. Merce was only a teacher's assistant, but one night he had Kennedy in his class. They became quite friendly. The future seemed bright and promising. Kennedy had on one occasion invited Merce to his house for dinner . . . and then, after dinner, had taken out his wallet and offered Merce Ite a twenty-dollar bill. Naturally Merce Ite had refused. Refused with a certain indignation that was tempered by the love and admiration he felt for the young man who was to become the country's President.

As always his brother Cas listened to the story, and so did his brother's wife, and so did the few, the very few who entered Merce's office. I was one of them . . . I wanted to talk to him about Bontemps, but instead listened to him speak about Jack Kennedy.

5

It is common knowledge by now that Geraldine had received a call from Mr. Frank Ol. It was a totally unexpected call. She failed to recognize his voice. Then, when she did, she promptly assumed that he wanted a cab. But Mr. Ol did not want a cab. She could see him quite clearly in her mind, resting his shoes on his desk, his secretary at his side. She could hear every word he was saying.

The words were familiar. They were there for everyone to use. Mr. Ol chose a certain combination. Everything he chose was quite deliberate, and done for a reason that would be consistent with what had preceded it. He asked her if Hank would be interested in doing some part-time work. Nothing strenuous. He was counting on Hank, he said.

Why didn't he call me, asked Hank. Why did he call you. What am I supposed to do. Did he pick me because of something you said. Have you been telling people that I do not like my job.

A week later, on a Tuesday, Hank left the plant together with his buddies. He declined an invitation to go bowling. He got into his car and drove to the Ite house. He was in no particular hurry and chose a circuitous route. Along the way he waved to a couple of familiar-looking people on the street. One of them recognized him, and waved back. I'm on my way, Hank said to himself. A bit further along he stopped at a public phone and called Geraldine. What's the matter, she asked. Are you all right. I'm just fine, he said. I'm driving to the Ite house this minute . . . In fact, I'm calling from a booth that's only two blocks away from their house . . . Just then Geraldine's other telephone rang, and she hung up on him.

Mrs. Ite did not recognize Hank. He may have been vaguely familiar looking, but she did not recognize him, or know his name. She also did not know that he was the former table tennis champion, or that he was married to Geraldine. When she let him into the house, all she knew was that Frank Ol had hired him to divide the second floor. Not knowing Hank it never occurred to her to wonder why Frank Ol had picked him, and not someone else . . . someone who was a carpenter, for instance. On their way to the second floor Hank caught a glimpse of the first floor. In many respects it was everything he had ever expected. The large oval table in the dining room had a deeper and richer gleam on its surface than the table in Hank's apartment. It was to be anticipated. In a sense, these differences went to the heart of the matter. From the second floor it was possible to overlook the entire lawn where the garden party had taken place each year. Bud, the son of Mrs. Ite, was seated next to a young man in the garden. Hank could see that both men, seated at a small round garden table, were in animated conversation. They were laughing a lot. They also looked incredibly relaxed. The drinks in front of them were half empty. Mrs. Ite had not offered Hank a beer. It had simply not occurred to her. Hank, standing at the window, taking in the scenery, noticed that both young men wore white trousers. He had worn white trousers the night he won the table tennis championship. I looked up and caught sight of Hank's face at the window staring down at us. I looked to Bud for an explanation. He's going to build the dividing wall for the new apartment, Bud said to me. I wonder why Frank picked him . . .

Who is he, I asked . . .

Just a town character . . . although at one time he actually was the local table tennis champion. At this we both burst out laughing.

I've heard all sorts of stories about his wife, Geraldine . . .

You must tell me more, I said . . .

6

The blueprints for the new apartment upstairs are spread out on the glass-topped table next to the window. According to the plan that was prepared by one of the younger men in Mr. Ite's architectural firm, the stairway to the second floor remains unchanged, but it has lost much of its former significance, since the new tenant will be expected to use the staircase at the rear. On the right, the library and Mr. Ite's study have remained intact. Mrs. Ite explained to Hank what she wanted him to do. Basically, she was repeating word for word what Mr. Frank Ol had told her. She had a retentive memory. She didn't even need to refer to the blueprints, she simply referred to Mr. Frank Ol's words. When speaking to Hank she avoided looking at his face. Instead her eyes were focused on the familiar upstairs wallpaper, on the cut crystal vase, on the long narrow table. She is fully aware that Hank is the instrument that will effectively change the familiar second floor. The furniture will have to be moved. She is not opposed to the change . . . she now, more than ever before, recognizes the extent to which she is dependent on Mr. Ol for advice . . .

You will need the additional income, Mr. Ol explained to Mrs. Ite. Mr. Ol can be extremely persuasive when he wants to be. Furthermore, Mr. Ol said, if you ever put the house on the market, it will fetch a higher price. All that is disputable. But she agrees. She is accustomed to agreeing. Still, there are so many unanswered questions. Why is her husband missing. Did he leave of his own free will. Is he still alive. She and her son Bud and the state police had searched for Mr. Ite for months and months . . . I'm sorry, the Mayor had told her, but Cas is a very thorough guy. He left absolutely no trace. No one had seen him . . . he never checked into any hotel, or took a bus, or a plane . . .

7

Hank is a neat and methodical worker. While constructing the wall his mind is already on the next phase of work to be done in the apartment. It is a pleasant change from driving a forklift. Dividing the upper story of the Ite house seems perfectly reasonable to him. One additional attractive feature of the new apartment will be the long balcony that runs the length of the wall overlooking the garden below. The new tenant will have a splendid view. He will be able to see Mrs. Ite almost daily. She is still young and attractive. She has a perfect smooth white skin . . . Infrequently Hank had seen her in the street without knowing that she was the wife of Mr. Cas Ite, the now missing architect. Hank has never inquired how his wife, Geraldine, came to meet Mr. Ite and Mr. Ol and the Mayor. Everyday people run into each other, people meet each other, people are introduced to each other. Mr. Ol introduced Geraldine to the Mayor, only he was not the Mayor at that time, and the latter introduced her to Mr. Ite, who in turn offered her a job . . .

In part, there is now in Hank's brain a clearer understanding of the surfaces that he finds so attractive. Years ago he pitted his intelligence, his ingenuity, his innate reflexes against a number of agile but faceless opponents, across the green surface of the ping-pong table. The table was divided by a low net. A great many of the boys now playing at the Y no longer recall Hank or his spectacular triumph at the table. He revisits the site of his former great accomplishment. He vacuously stares at the table, and then, still a bit lost, also stares at the large swimming pool, and at the white tiles in the shower. The surfaces present no surprise. He is quite free to move wherever he wishes as a former member of the Y, as long as he does not use the pool or the ping-pong table. In order to do that he would have to become a member again. Mr. Ite, the architect of the Y, had been an honorary member for life. When he designed the Y he anticipated the large crowds that would flock to certain events. He planned the swimming pool, the dressing rooms, the showers, the recreation rooms, as well as the large gym where the table tennis tournament took place.

Hank is still hard at work on the dividing wall on the second floor. Mrs. Ite seems quite satisfied with the rate of his progress. On occasion she is alone with him in the house, but it never occurs to her to feel nervous . . . it never occurs to her to offer him a beer . . . she is far too preoccupied with the shifting around of the furniture . . . At this stage she is still shifting the furniture around in her head. All the same, when she undresses at night, the topography of the interior has changed. Who will live here, Hank asks himself as he sands down the new door of the apartment upstairs. At the far end of the corridor are the doors to the library and to Mr. Ite's study. Both doors are always kept shut. On one occasion Hank has seen Mrs. Ite enter the library. She emerged a few minutes later with a book under her arm. There is a certain satisfaction, Hank discovers, in sanding down a surface. No one is rushing him, no one cares if he takes a few hours longer. He sits in the as yet unfinished kitchen of the new apartment and eats a sandwich that Geraldine had prepared for him. The interior of the apartment is freshly painted. The windows are wide open to let in the fresh air. On his overalls there are a few paint stains. Hank is munching his sandwich without even knowing that he is eating. Next Sunday he and Geraldine will drive to Pittsfield to visit Bontemps. They have bought Bontemps a new pair of shoes. Coming to grips with one's life, Hank has come to feel, is simply a matter of recognizing the surfaces that surround one on all sides . . .

8

I found the second-floor apartment freshly painted . . . it was bright and cheerful. I found myself at a complete loss, not knowing what to say. If I understood her correctly she was anxious for me to stay. Bud is so fond of you, she said. Until we find someone to take the apartment, you'll be extremely comfortable up here. But I don't need all this room, I said. You will, she said, once Bontemps and the film crew show up. On Monday I moved in. The apartment was no longer quite bare. She had moved a few pieces of furniture into the freshly painted rooms. I also received a key to my own entrance at the back as well as a key to the front door, just in case I ever found it more convenient to enter that way . . . The transaction was handled most informally. I'll expect to see you later this evening, said Mrs. Ite. I dropped in to see Mr. Ol in the afternoon. He seemed genuinely glad to see me . . .

9

Like Geraldine, Mrs. Ite had grown up in this town. Their paths may have crossed on more than one occasion. Both have taken the elevator to Mr. Ol's real estate office. Both know what the surface of his hard hand feels like. Mrs. Ite is pensively staring at her entire wardrobe, as she selects a dress for the evening. She is undressed. The hard surface of Mr. Ol's hand, or for that matter, of any other part of him, no longer has any place in her mind. At this very moment she is arranging in her mind the sequence that is to be followed for the next few hours. She will start the evening in one room, then move to another, and finally to a third. The evening is divided by the three rooms in her mind. This division is not arbitrarily arrived at. The events are to a degree influenced by the familiar contents of each of these three rooms. One of the three rooms is a bedroom. It is, however, by no means the only room that can be used for the purpose she has in mind.

We are lying side by side on the bed . . . we are both naked . . . Bontemps is a million miles away.

Are you afraid of Mr. Ol, I ask her.

Afraid? Why should I be afraid of my husband's oldest and dearest friend.

Then why have you had the front door lock changed?

10

Three years after his father's disappearance Bud Ite stumbled across the keys to his father's study. The study was located on the second floor next to the library. Its door was always kept locked. No one knew why, but Mr. Cas Ite always locked the door. I think, Bud said, these are the keys to father's study. Mrs. Ite studied them closely, and then agreed. Yes, they do look like the keys to the study. Where have they been all this time.

I was going through some of father's things, and found them . . . Mr. Cas Ite had been gone for three years, but the human brain does not really know what three years are. It cannot tell the difference between say three or seven years. It has no way of measuring time . . . it can only measure the receding glow of surfaces. I want all my films to be shot in bright color, said Bontemps, because he was afraid that they would fade in our memory.

I think I'm going to go up and have a look at father's study, said Bud casually, looking at us. There may be one or two things of interest in the study.

May I join you, I asked.

Why don't we all go up together, Mrs. Ite decided.

I'm so glad you're here with us, she said, as Bud opened the door of the study.

11

The farmers are waiting to sell more of their land at inflated prices. They are waiting for someone to build another Mall on Route 11. Like the former, it too will contain a bakery, a bank, four shoestores, a hairdresser, dress shops, a bookstore, five movie theaters, all under one roof to take care of our immeasurable needs. Sometimes, perhaps, to a half-filled house, one of the movie theaters will play a recent film by Bontemps, a film in bright color, a film about a man who is never seen on the screen. A film about a man who like so many of Bontemps's characters is shot or shoots himself . . . and is only found in his study three years later, the body partly decomposed, the weapon missing, but no one, not the Mayor or the Chief of Police, or any of the prominent citizens in the town wishes to create a fuss. Bontemps, who is not particularly interested in individuals, will simply use the dead man as a point of departure, I kept thinking as I sat next to Mrs. Ite in the large black limousine. Bud was seated in front, next to the chauffeur who was driving us to the belated burial of Mr. Ite. It was three years overdue. Afterward, with a broad smile, Mr. Ol introduced me to everyone as the young tenant staying at the Ite house, he referred to me as an assistant of Bontemps . . . Bontemps, you know, the French film director.

I admire Mrs. Ite's serenity as she faces Mr. Ol. He is the first to look away.

THE ISTANBUL PAPERS

PART ONE

There's simply no room for a reappraisal. Yes, it's late in the day for such an undertaking. Disconsolately I sit at my desk at the Consulate thinking about Norman and Jack. But why, I persist in asking my fellow attachés, is everyone obsessed with winning . . . so carried away by the exhilaration of making a touchdown, and above all, so desirous of marching down the corridors of power . . . Listlessly I invalidate a few more passports after scrutinizing the most recent blacklist from the State Department. I've become increasingly convinced that little can be accomplished without a thorough understanding of Mao's writings. As usual, I spend the late afternoon rowing on the Bosphorus. What peace, what serenity. I let the boat drift, while I recline on the seat and gaze into the azure-blue sky. In my heart I embrace all mankind. I think back to my carefree days at Harvard . . . of the three of us, Norman, Jack and I . . . our convictions as yet untested, and our enthusiasm not the least bit blunted by the guys who preceded us . . . who had gone through it all. We still lusted for the power and the fame that was rightfully to be ours. All of us unashamedly straining at the leash . . . ready to jump at the starter's whistle. How I must have let them down.

  In all candor, I owe Norman and Jack more than I care to admit. I owe them my upright stance, my bravado, and my fearless pursuit of human dignity. Norman and Jack used to go out together on double dates, while I remained closeted in my room with the second part of *Epistolae Virorum Obscurorum* by von Hutten, who is not to be confused with the Baroness von Hutten zum Stolzenberg, who was born in Erie, Pa., some three hundred and fifty years ago. I always preferred inward communication, and also read medieval French texts. What did Norman and Jack ever see in me? I like to think it was my power of suggestion, as well as my hearty laugh. A hearty laugh, my mother used to say, cleanses the air of all suspicion. My eyes mist over.

PART TWO

Those inward dialogues, I keep telling myself, must discontinue. I try not to slack off at work. Now all attention is upon Cuba, and the newspapers carry in full Jack's latest response to the unexpected missile threat. Hardly any mention of Norman these days. Poor forsaken Norman. Like me, he must be quietly fretting away in some dank room. One day, mark my word, we will startle the world. In my own small way I have contributed to the phantasmagoria of our collective glory by being kidnapped for the third time, and consequently making all the local headlines. AMERICAN ATTACHÉ KIDNAPPED AGAIN, it said in bold Turkish print. This time I was away for three days . . . three long fly-infested days in an octagonal-shaped room with bars on the window. The Embassy was quite decent about the ransom. As soon as they shelled out the $375, I was set free. Just don't make a habit of it, said the Ambassador, when I thanked him for his intervention. The turbulent experience certainly adds new dimensions to my understanding of Man. I seldom go out now without a Smith and Wesson in my hip pocket. To my surprise the kidnappers displayed little interest in my friendship with Norman or Jack. I expect they thought I was exaggerating. Istanbul is a hive of intrigue. Unfortunately, the Embassy library leaves a lot to be desired. But there are so many other rewards. I am carried away by the slow emollient pace of the city . . . by the magnificent mosques with their sun-baked courtyards . . . by the serene flow of the river, and by the shiny eager faces of the young boys who beg for a livelihood.

Seldom has anything so succeeded in inspiring me. Tomorrow I'm to meet Hitler's daughter. I have to thank Evans, the butler at the British Embassy, for the introduction. He is rather too fond of his Haig and Haig, otherwise we see eye to eye on almost everything else. There's to be no end to intrigue, I write my mother. Hitler's daughter, indeed. I didn't even know he had a daughter. How selective the eye can be, I brood as I watch a fly knock its silly little head against the windowpane. Can flies see through glass? My placid thoughts seek a release from the routine work I do . . .

PART THREE

What a formidable woman, what intoxicating eyes. Over Turkish pastries I chat with her about Rilke. The flawless Aryan profile is enhanced by her shoulder-length blonde hair. At present she's staying with two Turkish friends of Evans's. I do not examine this delicate situation too closely. All the same there's much that needs elucidating. How are your friends, Norman and Jack, she inquires. I stare at Evans reproachfully, and he has the grace to look ashamed. Can no one ever keep any confidences? We're hardly the closest of friends, I explain to Otilla. We went to Harvard together. You may have read accounts of our friendship in *Esquire*. Norman was the chronicler of our youthful high jinks. He and Jack used to go out on double dates. Sometimes they'd ask me to accompany them, but my studies compelled me to decline their invitation. Were you keeping yourself chaste, Otilla asks with a look of amusement. The word "chaste" does not sit well with me . . . but an unforeseen attack of abdominal cramps saves me from making an utter fool of myself. After all, why quibble over a word? Mao did not quibble when he undertook the Long March . . . or the broad swim. When I return from the bathroom I find that Evans and his two friends have left. Otilla speaks wistfully of the United States. It is a society where so much can transpire. You can say that again, I exclaim. She looks at me inquiringly, and then forthwith, in all innocence, obligingly repeats the remark. The poor dear. She too has many sad memories. One cannot help but be affected by them. Certainly, her days were not all butter and roses at the Wolfschantze. We sip coffee on a low divan . . . and hold hands. How serene the Bosphorus, and the slow gait of the throngs in the crowded streets of this resplendent city with its cupolas gleaming in the mercurial light of the late afternoon. I leave her side in the early hours of the morning. What will all my Jewish friends think of me? I can barely control my urge to sing in the shower after I get home at 5 A.M. My jubilation is firmly rooted in love. I've always known that one day I should meet a woman who would deserve my respect.

PART FOUR

Evans is nursing his fourth Haig and Haig. He has come over for a game of slapjack. To think that I've always stood in awe of English butlers. They are, I still believe, Britain's principal monument—its answer to Angkor Wat. Evans is no exception to the rule. His rigorous training has been of inestimable help to him as he forms snap judgments of each new international crisis. Otilla's falling for you, old chap, he cheerfully declares. If only she was someone else . . . if only Norman didn't feel such a passionate dislike of all Germans. After all, what is past is past. I keep urging her to write her memoirs, but she's only interested in cooking, said Evans as he pocketed his winnings. Before taking his leave he asks me if I happen to know any American publishers. Only the ones whose passports I have stamped, I reply stiffly. You realize, don't you, that we have an enormous responsibility towards her. Why, her recollections alone might drastically change the prevailing view of the Third Reich. But you just said that she doesn't want to write, I point out to Evans. Barely controlling his irritation, he coldly replies that that has never prevented anyone from being published. That night I dash off a short note to Norman. Hitler's daughter alive and well in Istanbul. I think I may be falling in love. Desperately need advice. P.S. Who is your present publisher?

PART FIVE

Receive back a stormy letter from Norman sent by special delivery. He threatens to publish it in *Partisan Review* unless I straightway submit it to the *New York Review of Books*. Hitler's daughter hasn't gone over too well with him. Some people can't seem to rid themselves of all that old film footage of World War II. It's that eye for an eye all over again. The remainder of the letter is devoted to Cuba. Norman insists that Jack intends to bomb downtown Havana. At times he can be laughingly childish. Bomb Havana! What next? I spend the afternoon with Otilla, rowing on the Bosphorus. She loves American cooking, and speaks reverently of pumpkin pie and chicken-in-the-basket. Her mother, a von Huttenau zum Kastanienvogel (no relation, of course, to Ulrich von Hutten, 1488–1523, author of the second part of my beloved *Epistolae Virorum Obscurorum*) had met Hitler at a wine festival in Salzburg. According to Otilla, it was love at first sight. At night I feverishly type twenty closely spaced pages about Hitler's favorite dishes. Evans introduces the only sour note by harping on my failure to stamp a visitor's visa into Otilla's passport. It could wreck my career. I prefer to follow the proper channels. He jeers at that. Don't you want to show them up, he asks, and stride shoulder to shoulder with Norman and Jack down the corridors of power? He's been reading too many novels by C.P. Snow, but he has also placed his finger on my Achilles' heel. My face turns white. I too think of the royalties her memoirs would bring. Enthusiastically I agree with Evans that she deserves a fresh start. I dash off another letter to Norman. I'm thinking of marrying Hitler's daughter. Please advise . . .

PART SIX

When together with Otilla I try to skirt the dangerous reefs of the past. The less said about papa, the better. I look deep into her stormy eyes, and see the tall fir tree forests of her Bavarian childhood. I detect Till Eulenspiegel in her dreamy smile. Oh, how I look forward to the merry pranks after lights out. I speak privately to the Ambassador's secretary, a hefty girl from Milwaukee. But she's appalled at the revelation of Otilla in Istanbul. Stay clear of her, she warns me. We don't want the wires from the White House to start humming. In the meantime Evans is becoming increasingly worried. The visitor's visa is not forthcoming, for which, according to him, only I am to blame. Things reach a head when Evans threatens me with my own unloaded Smith and Wesson. I laugh in his face. Go on, I taunt him. Pull the trigger damn you. We are both equally taken aback when he obligingly does so. After hearing the dry click of the unloaded weapon, Evans uncharacteristically breaks down and sobs. It is most embarrassing. Of course I forgive him. Early the next morning I receive a telegram from Norman requesting additional information. What is she like? Send photograph. I love Amerika with all my soul, Otilla confides to me. Slowly, hand in hand, an immense cavalcade of men and determined women proceed to climb to the pinnacle. Will I ever reach it, I ask Otilla. What is the view like from up there? The local newspapers are still full of talk about Cuba. Apparently it's to unleash or not to unleash the Air Force, that's preoccupying Jack. Will he select Norman as an eventual go-between, I wonder. Norman's heart, Jack always used to say, is in the right place. I know where Norman's heart is, I used to reply. It's his magnetic left hook that I'm worried about. But Jack would never hear any criticism of Norman in those sun-kissed days at Harvard. He was that sort of a person . . . upward bound, self-confident, heading for the center of the storm and the Presidency. I doubt if he ever chuckled over Diderot. Diderot could wait as far as he was concerned. In the final analysis my mother was right. Don't drift into corners, she said. Keep mingling . . . no one ever disdains a happy heart. If only I had payed attention to her advice. I often think of those hectic days, standing shoulder to shoulder with Norman and Jack in the quadrangle. Only their dreams have come true.

Of late I am surrounded by deep pockets of silence at the Consulate. Has word leaked out, I wonder. You and your big mouth, grumbles Evans. But he has not given up hope of persuading me to stamp Otilla's passport. I tell him that I need more time to think about it.

PART SEVEN

Will you take me to Amerika, she whispers, after I rapturously embrace her, and rain kisses on her unprotesting mouth. The presence of Evans and his Turkish friends doesn't inhibit my unexpected display of passion . . . quite the contrary, I find that it inspires me to fresh peaks of love and desire. I breathe in her Teutonic perfume. I can almost discern the rattle of drums in the background. Hitler Jugend be damned. If Jack can profess to be a Berliner, I don't see why I can't be the lover of Hitler's daughter. Will you marry me, I ask her. Upon our arrival in Amerika, she replies unhesitatingly. Women have always been able to twist me around their little fingers . . . their jewel-studded, adorable little fingers. Norman calls me unstable in his latest letter. Look who's talking. Norman is quite a pacesetter in instability himself. Otilla returns my volume of Diderot, *Jacques le fataliste et son maître.* There's a large butter stain on the dust jacket. I have only myself to blame for lending her the book. Otilla doesn't even once refer to the stain, something I find mildly disconcerting. I must admit that I now have second thoughts about our hasty engagement. What will my mother think . . . and Norman, and Jack . . . not to mention the State Department. But I keep telling myself that I mustn't be too harsh on Otilla. God knows what life must have been like in those bleak days of '43 and '44, surrounded by imbeciles like Goebbels and Goering. Without much success, I urge her to move into another apartment. Shyly she slips her passport into my pocket. I breathe a sigh of relief when I open it later and see that she uses her mother's maiden name, von Huttenau zum Kastanienvogel. All the same, I spend a sleepless night tossing in my narrow bed. The next morning I take matters in my hand and apply for a leave of absence. To my surprise it is granted immediately, no questions asked. I have come to recognize that one of my chief drawbacks is my failure to communicate the intensity of my feelings.

PART EIGHT

Evans, his two cronies and myself see Otilla off on an Air France jet. My worries are just beginning. I can get fifteen years for what

I've done. Even with a few years off for good behavior, it'll take me out of the race forever. Norman promises to meet Otilla at the airport. No snappy Nazi salutes, please! I caution him in my last letter. I spend the next day straightening out my desk at the Consulate . . . shake hands all around, and take off for a few days with Mother. Norman informs me, when I speak on the phone, that Otilla is staying in a furnished room in Brooklyn Heights. How would you like Hitler's daughter as a daughter-in-law, I ask my mother. She falls down in a dead faint, causing me no end of concern. Where is my heart, I keep asking myself while anxiously gazing at myself in the mirror. This has to stop. Four days later I fly to Washington. To my dismay Jack is curt when I ring the White House. No invitation to lunch. All the same he invites me over, and we have a long chat in the oval Blue Room. The responsibilities of the office he now holds has dampened much of his former enthusiasm. He seems less receptive, and hardly pays any attention to what I have to say about Turkey. Past friendships, I have come sadly to realize, soon turn into liabilities. Poor dauntless Jack, too loyal to discard the memories of our somersaults and headstands at the Harvard gym. Dutifully I put him into the picture about extending visitors visas for tourists from Turkey. When I mention Norman, Jack frowns. To think that I once considered him to be a friend, he declares angrily.

You mustn't take everything he says to heart . . . I mean, where would we be if we did . . . we'd be white Negroes, ha-ha. But Jack doesn't join in the laughter. If you must know, after Castro, Norman is my most vexing problem. I know better than to ask Jack to explain. You don't become President by explaining what you mean each time you open your mouth. I leave the White House, still musing over his last remark.

PART NINE

The following afternoon I visit Norman in his luxurious pad. He at once offers me a drink, after which we compare our lifelines, and wrestle on a Japanese mat. As usual he wins. I wish he wasn't so bloody infantile. I particularly resent Norman's smug look after he wins a wrestling match. When I mention having seen Jack the day before, Norman crows triumphantly. I beat him, he shouts. Always this insistence on beating people. It gets me down. I attempt to compose myself while he explains that he had threatened to turn all my letters to him, written on the Consulate stationary, over to the press the moment Jack ordered the bombing of downtown Havana. Former college friend of the President in love with Hitler's daughter now in Istanbul, would have made front-page news. You ruined my career, I howl. Go publish it in *Partisan Review*, he says peevishly, and refuses to give me Otilla's address. I leave with a heavy heart, nursing the ugly bruise on my chin where he hit me. Otilla, where are you? I place a number of ads in the personal columns of the *Village Voice*. I would never have suspected that so many women were named Otilla. Alas, none of the letters I receive are written in the spidery Gothic hand I have come to love.

Evans, forever an optimist, keeps sending me, care of my mother in Wisconsin, sections of the "Istanbul Papers," Otilla's purported autobiography. Such lies, such fantastic lies. He wants me to edit it and get Otilla to sign every page. Nothing I say will convince Evans that I can't locate Otilla. Norman gave Jack his word that if Havana remained unscathed there would be no scandal. But why, why, why, I keep asking myself as I gently bang my head against the bathroom wall. I have served my purpose, I suppose. I still find it difficult to believe that Jack would give in to Norman's threat . . . I have always maintained that Norman was an inflated windbag. All the same, not one bomb was dropped over Havana. With Otilla in his hand, who knows what Norman may next contemplate doing. I have not given up my search for Otilla. Once I thought I saw her leaving Schrafft's. I really don't think it was love after all. Yet I'm still upset by Norman's novel. All that talk about double-dating with Jack at Harvard . . . and I could only conclude . . . when I reached the part of dealing with the German maid that Norman was referring to Otilla. The sheer sexual perversity left me speechless. Worse yet, is he the sort of obsessional person who would practice what he preaches. Would he dare. I called my mother in Wisconsin to tell her not to read Norman's banal outrage. Will I ever reach the mountaintop? What is the view like from up there? But there's lots of time. I am being posted to Beirut next month. The "Istanbul Papers" sent me by Evans are under lock and key at my mother's house. She is keeping her fingers crossed that no one will kidnap me in Beirut. I wonder, will I bump into Norman when I finally reach the pinnacle?

FRANK'S BIRTHDAY

FRANK'S BIRTHDAY, PART ONE

They are lined up for the take-off . . . England is in the second
place. Ludmilla von Huttenau casually leafs through a pocket edition of Mao's selected speeches. So far there has been little of that
tumultuous and frenzied commotion one might reasonably expect
from a crowd this size. Ten thousand is the latest estimate I have
been given. Even the police at the rope barrier appear relaxed.
Quite a number of them are exceedingly handsome lads with
bronzed faces: still, I refuse to entertain any doubts about the Chief
of Police despite the numerous complaints that have come to my
attention. I will not have my loyalty put to a test each time a sub-
ordinate embraces one of the junior assistants. All the same, how
easily one's confidence is undermined.

Ludmilla leans to the left. Ah, dear Ludmilla, how I long to
crush you in my arms. Now she doffs her purple helmet, and the
blonde hair comes tumbling down to her adorable shoulders. Gra-
ciously she accepts the bouquet of white carnations from one of the
town officials and then, in front of thousands of witnesses, throws
them straight at me. Unfortunately the flowers fall short . . . We are
all a little troubled. The scenery is breathtaking. How perilously
close we have come to war. My public offer to resign has shaken
the capital. Man must surmount the threat of starvation. Man
should build more dykes.

The Germans are incontestably ahead in coining technical phrases. They will make the most of their advantage. We have to follow in their footsteps. We must firmly grab hold of the rotor blade. Ludmilla has blue eyes and delicate wrists. What is she like in bed, muses Frank aloud. England evidently is suffering from a bad case of nerves . . . It is not unusual for a contestant's face to turn red with excitement, but a sickly green? The English contingent shouts encouragements. We join in, but the tremendous roar of the engines drowns out our lukewarm cries of: chin up, and good luck chaps. From now on it is downhill all the way. The referee is a reliable soul. He looks at me expectantly, then raises the starter's pistol, pointing it skyward.

Strictly speaking we are all prepared for something to happen. Now the tension on the participants' faces is not to be believed. I look at the line of people waiting their turn at the public lavatories. A white-coated individual carries the full buckets out the rear door. Best not to inquire into the disposal of the contents of these blue buckets. The less patient ones head for the trees. How human we are, I murmur to Frank. Idly he speculates, how many more sunsets until the next revolution catches us in the knees. What we now need is a breathing spell. I interrupt his reveries to tell him that the race has started. Obligingly he turns his head. Life is so inconclusive. Will he be happy with the gift I bought for his birthday?

FRANK'S BIRTHDAY, PART TWO

Ludmilla's tragic death has cast a giant shadow over us all. I am to be one of the pallbearers. The cortege winds its way over the Alps . . . She will never see this majestic scenery again. Storm clouds gather . . . and the public lavatories are clogged. Humanity, once again, has been given a great deal to think about. In the evening I study the pincer movement. Nature abounds with fresh starts. It also abhors a vacuum. I move restlessly from one baroque building to another. I also install a new cabinet . . . I have no explanation for my listlessness. Tea with Mother on Friday. She suggests a change of uniforms, something perhaps more dashing with gold epaulets. I have come to depend a great deal on her advice. She treats me with her customary reserve. On leaving I brush her cheek with my lips.

Frank marks time. He is wary of tribunals. He accuses me of dignifying the harsh reality of political thought by my many references to Aristotle. What we need are more bulldozers and not roses . . . I overlook the deliberate slight. These gloomy days do not augur a good year. I wear my new sky-blue uniform to the studio. Only a handful of friends know that I have departed from the prepared text. I am not ashamed to weep over the air. Let our enemies derive what satisfaction they can from this ill-advised but all too human reaction. Europe give me your tears . . . I shall preserve them between the pages of Aristotle. There you go again, says Frank bitterly. His birthday is soon. I think I may buy him something else instead. France and Germany observe another day of atonement. By and large my speech is favorably received by the well-disciplined throngs in the nation's capital. Too fiery, writes Monclair in the *Express*. Even England listens to my admonitions. I receive the ambassador at noon. As usual he does not come empty handed. This time it is an exquisite torte. Only Belgium, oblivious of its past errors, refuses to participate in the discourse that is raging over the continent.

I castigate Frank, and refer to my voluminous correspondence with Mao. Let the anvil drop where it will, the hammer is raised, ready to strike. The gears of revolution are grinding slowly. The students build elaborate barricades. It makes it so much more difficult to get about the city. Fortunately we are well provided with victuals. Like most servants, my cook has his nose to the ground. Ludmilla's death may yet prevent another clash. At the club there is some talk of canceling the annual banquet. Frank takes me to task. Where are the dykes, he demands to know. Poor Frank, poor impulsive friend, he cannot shoulder my burden. This summer I intend to vacation without him.

War permitting I shall edit Ludmilla's correspondence with von Klausewitz's ninety-three-year-old niece . . . All kinds of things are being said about her as well, but I am determined not to be deterred by malicious gossip. The photograph of Mao on Ludmilla's mantelpiece is now in my possession. Eagerly I seek the truth on the Master's placid physiognomy. Genius, alas, can be a liability. I let the curator of our National Museum of Costumes read a few of my poems. Suddenly his bifocals cloud up. Shamefacedly he wipes the thick lenses, his reptilian face purified by an emotion too strong to suppress. You are a devout man, he tells me. A prince . . . A true

81

visionary, to lead us out of this morass. More cabinet meetings. The students request a revolution. I appeal to their better natures. Sullenly they disperse. This afternoon I have need to see my optometrist about a slight irritation in my eyes caused by the tear gas. It is too early to say if more public conveniences are the answer. Revolutions are not settled in a day. Frank cuts me in the coffeehouse on Sunday. Where are those splendid days of roses? I may, after all, decide not to attend his birthday party.

FRANK'S BIRTHDAY, PART THREE

At the conclusion of the speeches I draw Frank aside. I must see you alone, I whisper into his ear. The guests take their time, no one seems in any hurry to leave. I elect to wait in the library. The house is surrounded, but the men have received orders to keep out of sight. The 2nd Armored is ready to move at a moment's notice. Once and for all I shall clear the air tonight. My critics accuse me of being confused. I have been blind, not confused. I hear a sound outside the window, and draw the curtains, but it is only the Chief of Police clinging to the outside ledge. His chief virtue is his boundless energy. Deep inside my heart I know that nothing will change with Frank's death. Nations will continue to grind each other to death. Glumly I stare at the full-length mirror. All is vanity . . . but the remainder of the line escapes me. Dear old Frank, it has come to this, after years of friendship. If only Ludmilla was alive . . . her spirited laughter, her convivial nature, her flashing white teeth would have enabled me to cling to the future. Now the future is past. I place the box containing the gold cufflinks on his desk in front of me. There is a tap on the door. I have the inescapable sensation of confronting my past. I say: come in. It is only a servant girl come to tell me that Frank has been delayed. She does not wait for a reply. Can I count on no one to be punctual? Where are those days of roses? We used to go to stag parties, and watch blue movies together. Outside a startled cry is followed by a resounding crash on the pavement below. Voices from the street hurriedly summon help. I hear calls for a physician. It takes me several minutes to summon up enough strength to go to the window and look down. At first I can only see the broad backs of the policemen who have cordoned off the building. Although I am no longer as athletic as I was in my youth, I lean out of the window holding on to the frame with one hand. Directly below on the pavement, four people are standing in a semicircle around Frank, who is on his knees, his doctor's case at his side, examining the body of the former chief of police now lying in a pool of blood. Briefly Frank looks up, and our eyes meet. The ambulance is not long in arriving . . . I have had the presence of mind this afternoon to alert the hospital about a possible accident that was to take place this evening. Under the circumstances one can hardly blame them for jumping to the wrong conclusion. Life is so bewildering . . . I am so enmeshed in the turbulence, in the down pull, in the phosphorescent glow of our communal destiny. Frank chooses not to ride in the ambulance. He will follow in his car. I can have him stopped at the border, but he must know that I am incapable of such a move. In one of the desk drawers which I pry open I find his diary. Such lies, such staggering lies . . . about me, about Ludmilla, about my mother, about the world. I pocket the diary as well as the cufflinks, and leave the house a stronger man. At night I dream of fleshy angels. The next morning after an invigorating breakfast of orange juice and soft-boiled eggs, I summon our five engineers to the chancellery. They are immediately captivated by my idea. Dykes have become the order of the day. Gentlemen, we may have to tighten our belts . . . I laugh. But the engineers are a humorless lot. Now I have to look for another chief of police, as well as another personal physician. Where are you Frank, I miss you. In approximately a year's time you will read in the papers about the completion of the first dyke in a chain of dykes that will embrace our nation. Dear friend, I look forward to the day when nations, arms entwined, will skip to the top of the mountain. I shall be looking for your face . . .

The first volume of our youthful correspondence is to appear next month. Needless to say all references to the brothels have been deleted. On page one sixty-five I refer to our meeting with Ludmilla in a footnote. "It was love at first sight for the three of us. A love that sustained us through years of separation." Indeed, I have remained faithful to that love . . . Each time I catch a glimpse of the new Police Chief's cufflinks I am reminded of that night in the library, waiting for you. Life, I'm convinced, is inconclusive, and passion leaves much to be desired.

WITH BILL IN THE DESERT

PART ONE

We keep staring at the desert for hours on end. Implicit in our desire to locate the route over which we have traveled is also a longing to see what lies beyond the horizon line. In our case there's no urgency whatever in heading toward the objective, since everything, as we stand here, seems to pass us by. As may be expected, we are wearing aviator sunglasses to protect our eyes from the bright glare of the sun which dangles from a wire that is attached to the ceiling . . . But everything is quite makeshift . . . quite primitive, really, the way it should be. One need only stretch out one's hand to turn off the light . . . but we adhere to the strict rules of the desert . . . sunset at eight, and not a moment sooner. In the desert the sun sets abruptly. One moment it is light, the next you are stumbling about in semidarkness.

Are you afraid, Bill asks me.

We have known each other for a considerable length of time.

No, not really. Why do you ask?

What I said is quite true. There's little room here for the kind of fear one might experience indoors in the city. Both Bill and I contemplate starting a new city in the desert. Yes, really . . . There are a great many things that have to be taken into consideration when you build a city in the desert. For one thing, being in the desert, there's that constant preoccupation with survival. Everything one does in the desert can be attributed to a fear of running out of water, or losing one's place on the map, so to speak, and not being able to return . . . Even the most menial tasks, like cleaning the campsite, demonstrate this dependence. We take turns cleaning our campsite. Then there are the countless inconveniences of desert life . . . the sand, the occasional windstorms, the incredible heat which in no time induces a lassitude and apathy that is impossible to shrug off, the vile taste of warm water and the inadequate food . . . it probably takes years before one has adapted oneself to the exigencies of the desert. But the rewards are immense . . . Alone, the incredible emptiness that unfolds in front of our eyes each time we stand up on our feet. Actually to have infinity in one's grasp . . . to compress an awareness of each day's activity into the ever-changing undulations of the desert's surface. When the infinity beyond the horizon line is identical to what we can see in front of us, one can safely reason that infinity lies in our grasp. Elsewhere in the world it is winter and summer, and people keep falling in love with inescapable regularity. All my friends must be wondering where I am . . . I could be crossing the Empty Quarter, or the Atacama Desert, or the Dzungaria Desert, or the Arunta, or Simpson, Desert, or the Black Rock Desert, or the Painted Desert in Arizona.

There are just the two of us and the girl who comes to do our cooking. As I said before, it's very primitive. We eat out of paper plates, using our right hands to scoop up the food. Inge was amused by our lack of dexterity . . . while eating we make loud guttural sounds, and we listen closely to these sounds, repeating them over and over again. Why are we so infatuated with these sounds, I would like to know? Do they compel us to adjust our gaze upon what is most relevant for the moment? Do they remind us of the sounds camels make?

I have warned Bill that I would leave the moment I became impatient, the moment I experienced boredom . . . that was my only condition. To begin with I spent a considerable time each day thinking about my fiancée. Seeing her, again and again, as she arrived at the airport and came running toward me. She is only nineteen, and not yet aware that the desert terrain is as varied as each day's encounter with the mailman. I was attracted to her at first sight. She has long black hair and black eyes and is part Spanish, part Mexican . . . The day before I left her I explained to the best of my ability my intention of staying in the desert . . . her English is poor, and I don't know if she understood me. Everything goes on as before . . . the problems accumulate until someone solves them, or until they solve themselves. Instead of the deep blue sky, I now stare at a white stretch of ceiling. Like most things, it is filled with imperfections. I stretch out and I make myself comfortable on the floor. It is not too bad. Although I have kept my watch, I rarely check to see what time it is. We eat when we feel hungry . . . we eat when the girl comes to prepare our meals. We stare at the girl as she crouches over the alcohol stove. It is quite instinctive . . . the minute she crouches, we stare. I often wonder if my stare is like Bill's. His stare is not at all furtive. It is the stare of a man bent on acquiring information. This very moment he may be examining his hand with the same intensive curiosity. I cannot get over my fear that the blanket might catch fire. Danger is always present. One can never protect oneself from it. For example, there's the danger that with the 400-watt light bulb burning the entire day, the wires are carrying a heavier load than they were intended to, and might begin to smolder and catch fire. At night, huddled under our blankets we speak in near whispers, as caravan after caravan keeps threading its way in the darkness from one end of the desert to the other . . . In the morning, first thing after we wake up, Bill and I will thoroughly examine the terrain at our feet for evidence of their illicit crossing.

Shall we go for a walk, I ask Bill.

He mulls this over in his mind for a moment. He has to have time to think about it. His shoelaces are untied. In general, I suppose, we present a hopelessly forlorn appearance to people who set store by such things. I'm game, he says finally. How far shall we go?

Oh, a couple of miles . . . nothing too strenuous. We'll avoid the drifts. We need the exercise, we've been doing nothing but sitting here for days.

You're right. I'll leave a note for Inge just in case she comes in while we're away . . . what shall I write?

Just say we'll be back in two, three hours.

What time is it now?

It's a quarter past three.

Shall I write Inge, or dear Inge?

Does it matter?

Of course it matters, he says impatiently.

Why not dear Inge? What's the matter with "dear"? Or do you think she'll misinterpret the "dear"?

How can one misinterpret "dear"? It's simply a question of form.

Exactly.

We say dear to everyone.

Some people would miss it. If you wrote: Inge, we've gone for a walk. Back in two hours, Bill. It would sound blunt. Unintentionally blunt. Far more blunt than you intended . . .

Bill looked thoughtfully into the distance, that all too familiar emptiness. Then I'll just leave out her name. I'll just write: Back in two hours, period.

As you please.

I waited while Bill searched high and low for his pencil. Then he had to find a piece of paper that was just right . . . after that, the question was raised where he should leave the note so that it would catch her eye.

Prop it up against the stove.

No, I'll pin it down with the ladle.

Fine . . .

Or better yet, I'll pin it to the pillow. He laughed softly to himself. What do you think . . .

Why not . . .

Have you got a pin . . .

I don't think so, I said cautiously. I couldn't really remember . . . Perhaps, after all, I'll prop it against the stove. He looked at me helplessly. I liked Bill, because, despite his size, despite his initiative, he was so uncertain . . . so dependent on outside advice . . .

Bill has red hair and is six feet tall. He broke his nose last August when the horse he was riding stumbled, and threw him to the ground. His nose hasn't healed properly. It is slightly askew, and gives his face a somewhat quizzical look. Perhaps the look had been there all along only I didn't notice it. It is, as I say, a matter of hunting down imperfections. One invariably leads to another. At one time Bill was in love with Leni Riefenstahl. This should come as no surprise to anyone who has seen her superbly shot and edited film of the 1936 Olympics in Germany. Bill and I watch the film almost daily. No film I have ever seen can match it in suspense or drama. The imperfections or shortcomings of the athletes are stylized, as if the losers had spent all their time training to lose.

Tonight, I tell Bill, I think I'd like to watch the high jump events, the entry of the German team who raise their hands in the fascist salute, and the scene in which the Argentinian horseman flounders helplessly in the stream after having been unseated by his horse.

Do you miss Alva? Bill asks me.

How exhilarating it is to inhale the clear bracing air as the young athletes leave their bungalows in the Olympic village early in the morning and set off for a practice run . . . Naturally, Bill and I tend to have our personal preferences . . .

Bill repeats his question: Do you miss Alva?

When I start to cry, he awkwardly, but with genuine solicitude, pats me on the back, evidently regretting that he had mentioned Alva to me. She would spread her white arms and legs and lay back as if on a sacrificial mount.

I hope you have no regrets coming to the desert, says Bill.

I can always leave, can't I, I reply petulantly.

Bill turns away, obviously disappointed with what I said.

From the very start, Bill and I had decided to discard the calendar as irrelevant to our present way of life. After all, the desert negated time. It simply made no sense to burden our stay in the desert with an awareness of time that was perfectly useless to us. Our voyage, it must be clear, was a very stationary one, and our belongings only reinforced this. There was the tarpaulin which, attached by its corners to hooks in the wall, served as our tent, and the Riefenstahl film, as well as the movie projector which was continuously overheating, and finally, there was the desert, with all its unique discomforts. We were unarmed despite Bill's protestations. I was the one who had decided against weapons. On my last stay in the desert I had stayed together with a bunch of guys in what was a former fortification. We were all extremely jumpy. At night we posted guards all around the perimeter of the fortification . . . during the daytime we quarreled about who would stand guard and when. At sunset each day I would prime the dozen or

so hand grenades. I had come to enjoy inserting the three-second
fuses . . . not the actual procedure, but the fuss this entailed, since
everyone left the barrack for fear that I would blow myself up . . .

Bill keeps harping on my former stay in the desert. It is, in a way,
the only experience we have to go by. But by no stretch of the
imagination are we trying to revive, or worse yet, dress up the
past. Still, I must admit that I continue to dwell on certain details
of my stay . . . the discomforts were so different: they ranged from
the flies that would bite us to the sudden sandstorms that without
a moment's warning shrouded everything in a cloud of impenetrable
dust.

Did you get any mail, asks Bill.
Yes . . . every few days a Piper Cub would land with the mail.
Usually there was a letter for me from my fiancée . . .
Not your parents.
No . . . from my fiancée.
I didn't know you had a fiancée.
Certainly I did. Still have her letters.
Did you write her?
Oh yes, regularly. You can't expect to receive letters if you don't
answer them. Though there wasn't much to write about, as you
can well imagine . . .
What happened to her?
Well . . . they kept us too long in the desert. It wasn't as bad as
you might think. We had a canteen which sold soft drinks, choco-
lates, and beer. But the beer was of an inferior quality. It was a
label I have never seen again . . .
Were there any woman where you were staying?
Well . . . the canteen also served as a way station for the buses
and cars heading south. There were usually one or two buses a
week. Whenever a bus pulled in, we would descend from the fort
just to have a look at the passengers. They would sprawl out on
the folding chairs and hurriedly down a couple of beers, then the
bus would take off again. Once in a while there was a woman on
the bus, but generally she was accompanied by a man.
That was it?
Sometimes late at night we'd spot a light blinking in the distance. No one had the slightest idea of who it might be . . .

Your descriptions are so vivid to me, said Bill, sitting cross-legged on the floor, drawing the outlines of the city he was planning for the desert . . . I didn't think he'd keep on with it . . . The city had undergone a number of changes. Bill would spend a few hours each day working on the plan . . . it was slow work . . . The city I have in mind, he told me, should have easy access to the deep canyons . . . it will include a desert inn, a desert movie house, a large administrative building, and shops in an arcade, as well as a place where people can sell their produce . . .

A market?

Yes, a market . . . perhaps even a sports arena.

I nodded in agreement. Bill was very persuasive, and I never wished to argue with him.

Inge brought us our supper. She's only twenty-two and recently worked as a secretary. I don't know where Bill met her. Bill meets a lot of people. All he has to do is get on a bus, and he'll meet someone . . . Bill keeps complaining that Inge is too slow . . . he keeps calling her a cow, something that I resent. Of course, she does not measure up to Leni Riefenstahl. I expect Bill secretly had hoped that Inge, being a German, might evoke memories of Riefenstahl. Anyway, the less said about Inge the better. I don't know what Riefenstahl looked like . . . but it's not difficult to construct a picture of her: tall, blonde, large blue eyes, thin ankles and wrists, small breasts . . . perhaps a trifle masculine in appearance . . . certainly she would have the sense to play up her role . . . a sort of female desert fox. Inge has a snub nose, blonde hair, and blue eyes. But they are not frosty . . . I think she likes me. She does everything to comply with Bill's eccentric wishes, and even wears a desert tunic and desert shoes to please him.

How's your sex life, Inge? Bill asks her as she enters to remove the paper plates, and she, in no ways abashed, counters with: How's yours, Buffalo Bill? This broke Bill up. He kept laughing and laughing . . . I too join the general laughter . . . we have so few distractions here . . . so few things to laugh at.

What did you do today, asks Bill.

I suppose that Bill and I are accustomed to more secretive women . . . at any rate, to women who, whether it be true or not, seem to lead a second life which they keep from us. We are not terribly interested in Inge . . . Inge has become accustomed to being questioned by Bill. In fact, I think she likes to demonstrate to him her acute and critical eye, but her descriptions are too precise and factual. At ten, or thereabouts, she says, I took the Number 1 to Westwood. I was the only passenger, and the driver, a Puerto Rican, started to chat with me . . .

How do you know he was Puerto Rican, asked Bill.

Because he mentioned Puerto Rico when I complained about the cold weather. He kept saying that I should visit Arecibo . . . He came from Arecibo . . . they have fields and fields of pineapple out there . . . and then, just after another passenger got on . . . Inge laughed breathlessly . . . he asked me to go dancing with him this Saturday at the Casino . . . Dancing? Bill hooted, stamping his feet on the floor. At the Casino? Bill was enjoying himself. His laughter was contagious, and I felt myself being swept along. But where's the Casino, Bill yelled. I don't know, Inge shouted happily. For a brief moment we were united . . . the three of us by the geography of our determined laughter.

I think I'll sleep with her tonight, Bill confides to me.

What happened to your nose, Inge asked Bill . . . I tripped, he said, staring reproachfully at me. He had made no attempt to defend himself. I swung my fist at his face . . . restraining myself from repeating the same flawless arc with my hand. I do not like to contemplate change . . . it fills me with apprehension.

I watched Inge wet a handkerchief and hand it to Bill, who placed it over his nose. I was still counting on Inge to refuse . . . but who could refuse Bill? I did not refuse when he asked me to accompany him to the desert.

At eight the sun set, and the three of us were left in the darkness. They were speaking in whispers to each other. Before dropping off to sleep I thought I heard Inge solemnly say: I must warn you, I am not a plaything. I am not to be treated as an object. I felt curiously touched by her words . . . as if they had been intended for me and not for Bill.

Do you ever think about your previous stay in the desert, Inge asked me the following morning. She was lying on the blanket next to Bill, who was still asleep. She made no effort to cover her body . . . I looked at her the way I look at everything that lies in the middle distance, with somewhat startled unseeing eyes . . .

Did any caravans pass by last night?

She was trying to enter the spirit of the game. But when she lay down naked on the hot sand it was not at all like Alva . . . decidedly not. I still, sometimes, try to think of Alva . . . sweet, beautiful, mysterious Alva, who came from the country where the Aztecs plunged their stone knives into the chests of their hostages.

Today, says Bill looking at us, at me in particular, without the slightest trace of suspicion, today, we'll select a site for the city . . . He is on his feet, busy unrolling the plans, waving his hands, pointing to the horizon line . . . I think that Bill anticipated everything that followed. When Bill designed a city in the heart of the desert, it was for me, and no one else. The only thing left for us to do after the completion of the design, was to select a name . . . When Inge was out of earshot, we settled on Blitlu.

Inge keeps raging that we are ignoring her. She keeps making all kinds of unpredictable demands. Frequently we go along with her demands . . . and at night, Bill and I sleep with her. I am unaccustomed to making the necessary overtures, not out of shyness, but out of a natural reticence.

What is that over there, asks Inge in her very determined voice.

That? Bill shields his eyes with his hands as he stares into the direction she is pointing. That is too far away for me to see . . .

No, no, it's quite close . . . She keeps pointing into the distance. We feel somewhat uneasy when she points at the door. What is that?

What is what . . .

What do you call that wooden contraption that rests on hinges, and swings open when you turn the brass knob . . .

It's generally referred to as a door.

What is it doing here?

I'm going for a walk, I say to Bill. Care to join me . . . We walked in silence for over an hour . . . a silence punctuated by her shrill calls, her almost demented calls to us from far away . . . until finally the sun set, abruptly as usual, leaving us to retrace our steps in the total darkness . . .

Inge, shouts Bill . . . Inge! Inge!

I too shout her name, but our voices cannot hope to carry over these vast stretches of desert . . .

PART TWO

The second part of "Bill in the Desert" is about our trip to Blitlu, which is a picturesque oasis some four hundred kilometers from the ocean. The sky is blue and cloudless, and the sand drifts, long parallel ridges on either side of the straight macadam road, glint in the bright sun as we speed by. I keep trying to read a book of poetry Jackie had lent Bill. The poems are by Murssoyez, a black poet, who has spent most of his adult life in Paris, and now only writes in French. Included in the brief description on the book jacket are a list of his other books, but the book I'm reading, called *Return to Blitlu*, is the only one available in English. As the title indicates, the poems all deal with the desert. Murssoyez writes of his longing for the desert, and for the sight of his family and his friends, as well as his desire to be with his fiancée who is waiting in Blitlu. I continue to see in the bleak monotonous terrain which we are passing the ecstatic vision of Murssoyez, who dominates the desert around us with his evocation of joy as he, once again, holds his fiancée in his arms.

Mention is also made in the poems of many places we intend to visit. Bill and I are still wearing our aviator sunglasses, which have come in real handy on this trip. All things considered, we expect to arrive in Blitlu in three days. Once in a while we'll spot a bird, and this morning as we were getting ready to leave, Bill pointed to some animal tracks near the car. We are on our way to Blitlu by way of Ongaru and Mesola. Mesola is 200 kilometers out of the way, and it would seem that no one in his right mind would choose such a circuitous route to reach Blitlu. Mesola, today, is not even a town . . . Murssoyez mentions Mesola over and over again . . . Thousands of years ago it was the center of an ancient civilization, which was swept away by the desert. Now what is left of Mesola is a small group of rocky mountains that are riddled with caves in which Murssoyez claims his forefathers had once lived before they had begun to build the grandiose palaces and the elaborate monuments in the once fertile valley below. But the palaces and monuments are all gone, vanished, except for the pieces of shard and the cave drawings. In the early part of this century Mesola had still been a stop on the caravan route from Mougliot, but by the time Murssoyez was a young boy, the valley was deserted. Now, on this site, a French enterprise has built a luxury hotel with an outdoor swimming pool, and a restaurant that is described in our guidebook as being a three-star blend of East and West. That is why we are going to Mesola. Because Bill is demented . . . Because he must see it for himself . . .

Bill is half asleep at the wheel. He has no eye for the desolate terrain, or for the way the straight road splits our future in two. He sits hunched over the wheel, almost grown to it, staring at the speedometer, occasionally tapping it lightly with his index finger as he drives at a steady sixty-five, continuously attempting to break the speed record of the day before. He is pitting himself against the mileage marked on the maps we bought in New York.

Our nights are by no means comfortable, but by no means are they more uncomfortable than they had been in the past. We speak in near whispers as we lie huddled in our blankets next to the Land Rover.
How did Jackie come to invite you? I ask Bill.
She said, come and see me in Blitlu.
Just like that?
Yeah.
Did you tell her that you'd be bringing a friend along?
I wish you wouldn't keep asking the same questions over and over again, says Bill petulantly.

But what am I to do, since everything Bill tells me is totally unconvincing? I don't believe a word he says. I certainly didn't believe his explanation why Inge suddenly left us . . . and we had to cut short our stay in the tranquil desert . . . and I didn't believe him when he claimed to have run into Alva on the street, and that she had laughed hysterically when he mentioned my name.

I still think you should have been a bit more forceful with Alva, says Bill thoughtfully, looking at me.

What on earth do you mean, I ask coldly.

I think you should have explained your intention . . .

Intention? What intention? Now I was completely baffled.

Oh, go to sleep, he says.

Here I am, deep in the heart of the desert that may, at this moment, be present in the mind of a black poet . . . in the shape of a familiar map upon which a single journey can be repeated a thousand times.

Late the next day we stop in a small village that isn't even marked on our map. To our surprise it contains a small hotel that is run by an elderly French couple. The husband obligingly fetches his gun and bags a couple of birds for our supper. I try to talk Bill out of going to Mesola, but he is determined, and nothing I say will change his mind. He is taking speed, and it helps compress the great distances for him. He feels as if he has just started out. The couple who own the hotel are filled with questions. Where are you going? Who is the woman you are going to visit? How long do you intend to stay? When they see me reading Murssoyez's poems, they mention that he had passed through about a month ago. He was returning to Blitlu to visit some friends . . . At this I cannot contain my excitement. I keep thinking of his fiancée . . . see them embrace . . . Oh you know how it is with these blacks, says the wife of the owner disparagingly to me when I mention the fiancée.

All the way to Mesola, the next day, I keep thinking of Murssoyez's return. I keep speaking about it to Bill. One day, I too will return to my first fiancée, and then to my second . . . Unlike Bill, I have something to return to . . .

The sandstone cliffs of Mesola are steeper than I had expected. We drive over a dirt road into the valley. From outside, the hotel looks no different from the large and somewhat ostentatious motels that are springing up all over the United States these days. Bill parks our car next to a black Mercedes. Bill is disgruntled because Murssoyez has come between us. I change into a clean shirt while he inspects the carburetor and then the spark plugs. At least another half hour passes before he is ready.

So this is the famous restaurant, says Bill as we enter the large dining room. To our dismay we are the only guests. We are seated near a window, and during the meal we watch a short dark man in a white suit and a slim light-skinned woman dressed in a native costume, leave the hotel by a side entrance, and drive away in the black Mercedes. The waiter grins, and for our benefit makes an obscene gesture with his hand. The meal we ate came to forty-five dollars. It is the most expensive meal we've ever had. We did not want to leave any food on our plates, and when we left the restaurant we were both feeling ill. I suppose we were unaccustomed to eating so much. Bill was the first to throw up . . . Afterward we are both enormously dejected. At my suggestion we drive a couple of miles in the direction of Blitlu before bedding down for the night.

Bill flares up every time I mention Riefenstahl. He's becoming incredibly sensitive to everything I say. I cannot resist taunting him: Well, Bill. When are you going to build your city in the desert? Every few hours Bill compulsively checks the oil, the tires, and the water. He does not any longer complain when I read Murssoyez's poems out aloud at the top of my lungs.

The next day we reach Blitlu. On the outskirts are the usual whitewashed mud huts. I cannot contain my exuberance and excitement at being in the heart of Murssoyez's country. The black men and women are tall and good looking. The women wear brightly colored robes topped by an elaborate headdress . . . In the inner city the houses are larger, also white, with tall shuttered windows . . . and the streets are paved. Everyone we speak to tries to be helpful, one passer-by beckoning to another to have him confirm the information given us, until finally we are surrounded by eight or ten gesticulating men. She lives in the northern section, said a shopkeeper who spoke English . . . but we promptly lost our way, and were heading back to the center of the city when I spotted a large blue sign, which read: A Monument De Murssoyez . . . Deuxième A Droite.

The monument, a cylindrical polished reddish stone, stood in a small square. There was a low padlocked iron fence around the monument, but the gate was open, and inside the enclosure, when we arrived, stood a young woman. She was the first woman wearing Western clothes we had seen in the town . . . We watched as she placed some flowers at the foot of the stone. I could not read the inscription because it was in Arabic. Although the monument looked as if it had been recently erected, I still failed to connect it to Murssoyez, the poet.

Can you help us, Bill asked the young woman as she was leaving the enclosure. She spoke English with a faint trace of an accent . . . When we explained our predicament, she suggested that her husband might be able to help us. He knows everyone, she said . . . She sat next to Bill in the car, giving him the directions to her house. Blitlu, it appears, is much larger than we had expected. The northern section where she lives is by far the most attractive. Large villas surrounded by groves of palm trees . . . I mention that I had been reading Murssoyez's poetry, and wondered if the monument, where we met her, was put up for a relative of the poet . . .

No, she said. The monument is for the poet Murssoyez. My husband had invited him to stay with us. We hadn't seen him in years. He died the day after his arrival . . . It was a most terrible tragedy.

When by dinnertime her husband had not showed up, I suggested that we either continue our search for Jackie, or find a place for the night, but she insisted that we remain . . . and after dinner had a servant show us to our room.

Much later that night I whisper to Bill: Isn't it bloody strange?

Why are you whispering, he wants to know.

Because the walls are paper thin, and every word I say can be heard in the next room.

What were you saying, he asks absent-mindedly . . .

Why did she ask us to stay?

I see nothing strange about it, says Bill. He is preoccupied with his own problems. He is worried that someone will tinker with or steal the Land Rover.

The next morning we meet our host, who is the man we saw leaving the hotel in Mesola. He asks us to call him by his first name, Henry. His wife's name is Ella. Henry smokes a large cigar, while listening with half closed eyes to the description of our meeting with his wife. I'm certain he must know that we've seen him in Mesola . . . You are looking for Jackie, Henry says to Bill. Bill says Yes, and Henry tells him that Jackie lives close by. Only ten minutes by car . . . but she's away in Corsica. Henry smiles at our obvious disappointment. I know Jackie quite well. You see, she rents her house from me . . .

Well, I say finally. We saw the great desert. We ate at the three-star restaurant . . .

But did you see the cave drawings, inquires our host politely. No, we were too tired . . .

When I mention how distressed I felt to hear of Murssoyez's death, Henry abruptly inquires if Bill and I were at all familiar with Murssoyez's work. I show him the translation I have been reading, but Henry makes a motion with his hand, dismissing the book. Ah, that was one of his early books . . . You must read the later poems . . . He leaves the room, returning with two slim volumes of poetry, handing one to me and one to Bill. Somewhat shamefacedly, I admit that I do not speak French . . . What? Henry with a look of exaggerated astonishment stares at me, then turns to his wife, saying, Perhaps Ella will translate some of them for you . . . tonight!

That night Ella comes to our room. She is wearing a long white nightgown . . . She perches herself at the foot of my bed, which happens to be next to the door, and proceeds to read Murssoyez's poems. First in French, and then slowly and somewhat hesitantly, translating them into English with some assistance from Bill and me. We both feel acutely uncomfortable about her presence in our room, and keep looking at the door, as if expecting Henry to burst in at any moment. The later poems, just like the early ones, deal with the desert. Again and again Murssoyez mentions Mesola . . . he also mentions his fiancée, and the woman he loves. But I'm by no means certain that they are one and the same.

Later, much later, speaking in whispers in order not to wake Bill, I tell her about our former stay in the desert. Not my first time, but the second time together with Bill and Inge . . . I feel so tired, so very tired, she says almost apologetically, as she lies down beside me. The next morning Bill asks me if we had made love. When I refuse to tell him, he angrily leaves the room, slamming the door shut behind him.

After breakfast Henry drove us in his black Mercedes to the

villa Jackie rented from him in the winter. It was a modern stucco building with a large terrace and a swimming pool. The pool was empty.

Had Murssoyez met Jackie, I ask Henry.

Oh yes. He was a great women chaser. I believe they met in some salon in Paris . . . Then, his eyes narrowed as he stared at me: By the way, he asked, did my wife come to your room last night to read some of Murssoyez's poems?

I don't know if the panic I felt that moment showed on my face. Yes, I said after a brief pause. Yes she did . . . She translated a number of them into English.

Excellent, said Henry. But I cannot read the expression on his face and don't know what to expect. Had he at that moment pulled a knife on me, I think I would not have been the least bit surprised . . . instead he smiled.

Deep in my heart I know that I do not regret the death of Murssoyez . . . After all, Murssoyez has provided the adventure. That evening I tried to engage Ella in a conversation about Murssoyez. Henry is really the man who can answer all your questions, she said, and attempted to laugh. Henry, forever the attentive host, instantly launched into a number of amusing anecdotes about Murssoyez . . . most of them dealing with Murssoyez's love life. You must understand, said Henry finally, Murssoyez was a fine lyrical poet . . . nothing exceptional, but a good poet with a rather narrow range of interests . . .

Why do you keep belittling his achievements, asked Ella in a quiet voice.

My dear, I hope I haven't left anyone with that impression.

You published his books . . .

Of course . . . certainly . . . and he's a fine poet. But he was also, you will admit, something of an opportunist. He would attach himself to people in society . . . he was a good conversationalist, and would intrigue them with stories about the desert . . . But personally, he shunned the desert. He hated the discomforts, the heat, the flies, the privations . . . In Paris he was an exotic creature . . .

Excuse me, said Ella stiffly, and left the room. She gets tired so easily, explained Henry in his bland manner.

Later that evening Henry with great pride showed us his collection of Murssoyez's manuscripts and books. I counted seven books, in addition to several luxurious limited editions bound in leather. His work has been translated into nine languages, said Henry. I believe I have all the translations as well . . . you see, Ella and I were his oldest friends. I was the first man to publish his work. We were very close . . .

Before going to sleep, Bill went outside to have a look at our Land Rover. Someone, he discovered, had let the air out of the tires. I'll see to it first thing in the morning, Henry assured us.

An hour later Ella came to our room to read more poems to us. This time she slipped into Bill's bed. I hastily threw on a pair of pants and a shirt, and left the room. Henry was sitting in the dark on the terrace, smoking a cigar. Ah, he said. You've already tired of the poetry?

Yes, it's a bit heady, I replied . . . We spent an hour or so talking about Murssoyez. How did he die? I asked him.

He was killed by the brother of his fiancée. She had been waiting for him to return all these years. I believe it must have slipped his mind . . . he had so many women . . . besides, the marriage had been arranged by his parents long before he left for Paris. I feel I am partly to blame for his death since it was I who had invited him to come to Blitlu . . . He was stabbed not far from here. All of Blitlu was present at the funeral . . . I don't think I would be wrong in saying that among all the townspeople, even the ones who have never read any of his poems, there is a deep reverence for his work. I can't explain it. So with contributions from rich and poor, we put up the monument to his memory. People like you and Bill will pass it. You may never have heard of Murssoyez before, but by the time you leave Blitlu, you will never forget him . . .

Who is the woman Murssoyez refers to in his later poems?
Murssoyez was in love only with himself, replies Henry firmly.

The next day Henry took us to meet the mayor of Blitlu, a large friendly man who greeted us by saying: Ah, here are the two Land Rovers . . . Ha ha ha. Bill heatedly replies: Yes, and some bastard let the air out of our tires.

Apparently someone would like you to remain here, says the

mayor continuing to laugh. The mayor's house is not as splendid as Henry's . . . It is situated near the old city, and all the rooms are much smaller.

Did you know Murssoyez, I ask the mayor.

Of course I knew him, he replies. Everyone in Blitlu knew him. That's why we put up the monument.

At dinner we ate lamb and rice, washing it down with trintola, a locally made alcoholic beverage. Henry and the mayor would frequently translate snatches of conversation, since none of the mayor's friends spoke English. Before we left, the mayor introduced us to his young daughter. I recognized her at once as being the young woman who had left the hotel in Mesola together with Henry. She spoke some English, but was extremely shy . . . When I mentioned Murssoyez, Murssoyez having become the chief topic of my conversation, I saw the tears well up in her eyes.

She was to have been married to Murssoyez, explained her father after she had hurriedly left the room. He was on his way to the wedding when someone knifed him . . . When we find the man, we will kill him. Henry, who was standing at my side, seemed quite unconcerned by the seeming contradiction between his and the mayor's version of Murssoyez's death.

I think we better be on our way.

Yes, yes, immediately, says Henry.

No, I mean Blitlu.

Tomorrow morning I'll have the tires fixed, he promises.

But the next day the spark plugs are missing. That evening the mayor brings his daughter to dinner at Henry's house. She seems far less restrained . . . I speak to her about the desert, and about my previous stay in the desert. When I stare into her large black eyes I can see the murdered Murssoyez staring back at me.

I hope we shall all become close friends, Ella says to me that evening. But that night she does not come to our room, nor does she on any of the following nights. The days pass quickly. One day the mayor comes over in his jeep and takes us on a tour of his property, which is quite extensive. I thought you would like to see what I own, he says enigmatically. It is hard not to develop a liking for him.

In the desert sunsets are abrupt. One minute it is light, the next you are groping around in the dark. Other transitions, namely departures, can be just as abrupt. We all stand at the entrance to the house seeing Bill off. The Land Rover is filled with odds and ends that Henry and Ella have given him. Just before leaving, Bill hands me the sketches of the city he is planning to build in the desert. I have nothing to give him. I am wearing a native costume, and look as if I have lived here all my life. Even the English I speak has come to sound more and more foreign to me.

That afternoon, when Ella inquires if I had asked the mayor's daughter to marry me, I know that I have finally reached the center of the desert where people understand the needs of my heart.

NOTE: *"With Bill in the Desert" was written shortly after I saw a one-man show of Terry Fox at the Reese Palley Gallery in New York. Fox had placed a large square canvas, of the sort used in construction work, on the polished wood floor at one end of the 20' x 80' interior, and hung another five feet above the floor, creating a tent-like structure. In the well-lit, bare, white, windowless room the glare from the single bright lightbulb dangling from the ceiling above the stretched canvas defined the area of shade beneath it. The light formed a topography of the interior that was, at once, a familiar romantic configuration in which the tent became the emotive key to a kind of disturbance of things past, and another in which one's physical presence, one's emotions, were measured (and partly activated) by one's proximity to that light.*—W.A.

THE SECOND LEG

1

Ludmilla is wearing a purple dress which leaves most of her back exposed. I trace the letters L...O...V...E... on her back, but she fails to respond. She's not to be trifled with. Love, I ruminate, has become altogether dispensable. I broach her first meeting with Victor.

You were by yourself?

No, I was with Frank.

Ludmilla finds it difficult to believe that I have never been to Turkey, Egypt, Saudi Arabia, or North Africa. Then how do you explain your inveterate fascination with mosques, she asks. I have every confidence in my capability to avoid becoming senselessly embroiled with Ludmilla over such a trifling matter. I don't deny that Ludmilla has her life cut out for her. Mosques, however, are strictly part of my turf.

Ludmilla's distinctive turf is insidious sex. Invariably she discusses the pulse-beating tribulations of each horrifying encounter with her secretary, or one of the young assistants at the museum. They customarily listen with bated breath while Ludmilla describes her reactions, her indescribable multitudinous responses to the abrupt, crude, lascivious, blunt, and obscene proposals made to her in taxis, in subways, on escalators, in grounded elevators, and in a dentist's chair. One man insisted on trying her hands to the chandelier . . .

Breakfast
Breakfast
Breakfast
Breakfast
Breakfast
Breakfast

Breakfast takes forever: I point to a stain on her Bonwit Teller dress. Hastily she leaves the table. I can hear the water running in the bathroom as she rinses it with soap and water. Now it is one hour since she's left the table. I have only myself to blame for pointing out the stain . . . I cling to the reassuring sound of running water. There's much I can do to pass the time. For one thing, I plan my day in the city . . . In ten more days I'll return to Paris. My worst fears are confirmed when I reach the bathroom door. It is locked from the inside. I rattle the doorknob . . . I tap on the door . . . I overcome my timidity and call her name. I think I can hear voices. They are calmly discussing me. They have my measurement, all right. But what are they doing while discussing me. I am to blame for pushing her into this. I should have known that Victor would be lying in wait for her. All those courses in psychology have not prepared me for a locked door. I debate whether to force it open. It might only be jammed . . . I return to the dining room. I nibble at a half-eaten toast. I plan the next day, and the day after the next. Ludmilla couldn't remove the stain, so she had to wash the dress . . . and with one thing leading to another, she then washed her hair. With her head submerged under water, she couldn't hear me . . . Now she runs past me into the bedroom to change into dry clothes. She is not wearing the dress. She has, instead, wrapped a large towel around herself. I dare not approach the bathroom for fear of what I might discover. She has no time to put on her make-up. She leaves in a hurry. My inability to love has downright unsettled me. I can hardly pursue the most trivial task without being dejected. Love has embraced me to its bosom, pinioned me against the wall, and with an earth-shattering and resounding crash, hurtled me skyward against the light grey ceiling of the bedroom. Love has rejected all my claustrophobic demands.

Victor does not wish to offend me. He remains closeted in the bathroom until his hair has dried. I accept his matter-of-fact explanation that he suffers from a nervous stomach.

2

I musn't overreach myself. After an absence of four years, I return to New York without any apprehension that I might encounter my former wife. I saw her last week, said Ludmilla, when she and Victor met me at the airport, and then dropped the bombshell that she had offered to redecorate Alicia's house . . . It needs a new lease on life, she said maliciously. I content myself with listing the recent changes in my personality. For one thing, I'm no longer suspicious. No longer suspicious. Last night I dreamt of fleshy angels . . . that rules out Ludmilla. All the same she continues to dominate me and set the pace. I put it down to her singular lack of forbearance. She promptly begins my visit by asking me to prepare breakfast. She also tells me to stop being so complacent. Within four hours of my arrival she is being screwed by Victor in the bathroom, and any complacency I may have had is thoroughly shattered . . . But all this, considering my short stay in New York, is so much lead under the floorboards.

Ludmilla is exhausted. The exhibition of eighteenth-century costumes is to open in less than a week. Ludmilla says that everything has gone wrong. She requires sympathy . . . she also demands undivided attention. She asks me to fix her a drink. Resentfully I do as I'm told. She has another stiff drink, and then I ask her about Frank. No shilly-shallying about. I come straight to the point. Why did you leave Frank?

Oh, I just walked out on him. I couldn't take it any longer. He insisted on holding my arm . . . For hours on end I would only have the use of one arm. Life became so castrating. Finally, I was so fed up that I told him about Barcelona, Alicante, and about our encounter in Paris. I was so tired of his fucking deviations . . .

But Frank has his fingertip on the pulsebeat of time, Ludmilla says bitterly. All his business ventures are boldly executed, and well financed . . . His consistent bold approach, especially with young women, rules out any indecisiveness. Yes, his entire wardrobe of bold checked suits is an extension of this programed performance. Only when it comes to sex does he begin to falter. I suspect that Frank misses the bold checked suits and the bold checked underwear . . . He can't, says Ludmilla wistfully, adjust to his own nudity.

He even took Victor's in his stride. But the instant he loosens his belt buckle, metaphorically speaking, he is in a total funk . . .

The telephone rings. It is Victor. He tells her not to wait for him. He's been delayed. Oh, all right, she says despondently. She hangs up, and pensively bites her lower lip.

Victor. Age: thirty-two. Hair: blond. Mustache: none . . . Identifying marks: none that I know . . . Color of eyes: blue for dispassionate lust. Victor has the perfect build for an eighteenth-century courtier . . . as well as the enlightened dumbness, the dumbfounding dumbness that remains entirely unnoticed in bed.

Initially it was rather unnerving, says Ludmilla. With great sobriety, Victor would give me conflicting advice and stare at my lovely breasts. Later I would let him peek down my blouse. He began to grow on me. Yet I had no intention of making him my lover . . .

I do not wish to explore Victor's sex life with Ludmilla. As it is, Victor's unsettling habit of entering the toilet when it is occupied, or the bedroom when Ludmilla and I are in bed, speaks for itself. One feels free to speculate about the origin of his stealthy approach, about the origin of his peculiar accent, and of the massive college ring, of the natty ties, and of his prematurely aged face with his harried nearsighted look of hard determination, and of the short-lived flashes of lust in his speculative blue eyes whenever his gaze settles on Ludmilla's leg, not the deformed and misshapen one, but the other . . . or could I be mistaken?

Ludmilla strides up and down her bedroom. She's in a foul mood. The panties have flowers on them. She discovers a rip in one of her stockings and hurls it at the wall. She's had a trying day. The Fontainebleau costumes borrowed from the Louvre are coming apart at the seams. She shouts: I must get out of this hole.

3

I come to New York fully prepared for maneuvers. Thus far nothing's lost. The flesh will always yield to carresses, but the mind remains as obdurate as ever. It will take more than the combined efforts of Ludmilla and Victor to unsettle me. I will not be agitated, Ludmilla's histrionic efforts to the contrary, by her references to her two week's stay in my place. Her appeals to my sentiments are too forced to be genuine. I have concluded that she refuses to relinquish the description of my room in Paris because it pleases her to think of our meeting, two years ago, as the first of a number of unsuccessful attempts to break away from Frank. Victor claims that this apartment as well as the Italian sports car she drives belong to a dear friend. I can only think of Frank. Her magnificent leg, the one that is not deformed, continues to exercise its power over me. I will always stand in its shadow. How obsolete the heart has become.

4

The day after my arrival in New York I speak to her about Frank. At first she will only say that he misused her. I soon made the discovery that Ludmilla does not in the least object to being used . . . that is to say that she welcomes it . . . however, Ludmilla will not tolerate intellectual misuse. She remains firm on that. She's also unduly argumentative about it . . . One does not toy with a woman who possesses one misshapen leg.

Use or misuse, I am informed, is to be energetically applied. Ludmilla may even have a certain amount of physical disrespect in mind . . . An hour or two can always be set aside for that purpose.

If you like, Victor or you can misuse me after dinner, between a quarter of eight and bedtime . . . unless I have made other arrangements for that evening. She also volunteers the following: Frank studiously misused her superb talents and distracting figure with its one smashing leg, by largely ignoring them, except on one or two occasions when it suited his purpose.

I have just arrived in New York after four years of living abroad. I do not quite know what to expect. I am given to understand that Ludmilla does not expect any surprises from me. In nine days I shall return to my room in Paris. Fuck surprises. The first day back I shall sleep until noon . . . I shall forget the inequities that led to my shameful surrender to her demands. Dear Ludmilla has lost none of her former bounce.

START AT THE BEGINNING: Victor drops us in front of the apartment building where she is staying. She lights another cigarette while I struggle with my two valises. I follow her into the building. She steps into the elevator . . . and presses herself into a corner, breathing deeply . . . Her mouth is open, and the thin lips are unaccountably shaped into a tiny elongated O. A residue of fear clings to my perspiring palms. I have forgotten how large her mouth is . . . completely overlooked the size of her mouth as I was planning my visit to New York. So far she has not made one single reference to sex. It must be my imagination . . . my restless, troubled mind that is plaguing me. I remain alert. I place the large valise on the elevator floor between my legs . . . She presses the elevator button, then darts back to her corner where she grips the flat aluminum handrail that is attached to the wall at about the height of her waist. It must be my imagination . . . all the same I can hear her quite distinctly enunciate the ejaculatory words: fuck, balls, cunt . . . My vision blurs. My love is so deeply submerged that it will never surface again.

At most my interest in the apartment is only a minimal one. Naturally objects fall into view. I take note of the two built-in closets . . . the antique escritoire . . . the Moroccan rugs, as well as the record player that belongs to Alicia. I bought it for her birthday several years ago. Most likely Alicia replaced it with a more expensive one. I remain calm, diffident, entirely unaffected by this sad memory. It is so much more difficult to hide things in a modern apartment . . . there are fewer recesses, fewer niches, fewer false ceilings. There is a white extension phone in the bedroom. Instead of drapes or blinds there are wood shutters . . . but they are a far cry from the ones in my room. I change into a fresh shirt in the bathroom. I keep telling myself that I'm off to a good start . . . it is imperative that I believe this. Much to my annoyance all my shirts are badly wrinkled. One is so easily discomfited by any untoward experience.

I leave the bathroom door open . . . I continue to talk to Ludmilla. She asks me about my work, but from her disinterested voice I can tell that her mind is on other things. How quickly I have adjusted to her clipped authoritative manner of speaking . . . and to seeing her undress. She steps out of her dress. Now with both hands behind her back, she searches for the fastener on her bra. The effort this takes is visible on her face. From where I stand it appears as if her hands had been pinioned to the wall behind her. This does not strike me as the proper occasion to demonstrate my ebbing affection.

I'm so glad you decided to come, she says finally. But don't for a moment think that we can start exactly where we left off . . . I'm not at all certain what she means . . . I don't ask her to elucidate.

You don't mind our not being alone, do you?

I have the odd and inexplicable sensation of being trapped in this apartment. Now she examines her face in the full-length mirror, and shapes her mouth to form the letter O. Victor is in the next room. I can only assume that he has let himself in with his own key.

All evening I master forbearance. I decline to inquire into their true relationship. Why should it matter to me, a kind of stretched-out week-end guest, what she and Victor do in the bathroom. It is so simple to jump to an erroneous conclusion. First Victor excuses himself, and leaves the table. Then she goes to the kitchen to fetch the dessert and coffee. Don't run off and desert me, I say jokingly. The next thing I hear is their boisterous shouts, their unabashed shrill laughter. They do nothing to restrain their mirth . . . or the sound of running water. It is seeping through from under the bathroom door when I get up to investigate. I keep myself in check and do not bring it to their attention. All things considered . . . not to overlook the soaked bedroom slippers, as well as the inexplicable presence of the two damp pillows on the toilet seat. I am at an utter loss for an explanation. Is this all being done for my exclusive benefit. I am resolved not to take too dark a view of all this horse-play.

In place of bamboo blinds on the window there are wood shutters. It is not quite the same thing. Still it is a pleasant apartment, conveniently located near the park. Above the striped ocher and blue-green couch hangs the framed antique map of Paris I gave Ludmilla as a farewell present. Upon closer examination I notice a tiny X made with a red pencil marking the street where I had lived at the time Ludmilla and I met. The map affords me no pleasure. I would as soon not see this memento of her stay in my former room. In my mind I return to the bookstore on the Left Bank where I first came across the book containing the illustrations of the Great Mosque of Kairouan. Again, walking barefoot, I cross the immense courtyard.

Now Ludmilla joins me in bed. She is lying on her right side, and her good leg is rubbing up against my knee. The lights are out in the living room. But where is Victor. I seek solace in her damp arms . . . She rubs her deformed leg, like a cricket, over my sensitive skin . . .

Don't worry, she whispers. He can't hear us.

Why hasn't he left?

She carefully considers my question: He's handy to have around.

In what way. I brace myself for the worst.

In every conceivable way.

It is more than two years since I have been caught in the viselike grip of her misshapen leg. Her soft laughter passes through the stalks of green grass like a fresh breeze on a June night. Cautiously I raise her unblemished and perfect leg, and press it against my chest. She keeps it in that position with the aid of one arm.

Later I return to Victor's presence in the apartment. She keeps having nightmares, she tells me. Each night she revives her secret terrors. She awakes screaming. It helps if there is someone in the apartment to hold her hand. I keep falling asleep while she speaks . . . while she describes her nightly attempts to postpone the harrowing experience . . . In her dreams she disguises herself. She comes dressed as a priest, as an airplane pilot, as an agronomist. I remember little of what she tells me. She mentions the gravel path and the magnificent scenery . . . she crosses the alps on a sled. Her terror is a well-balanced act of self-destruction. She lacerates the people who surround her in her dreams . . . she maims and decapitates them in order to buy more time for herself. She invents fresh horrors in order not to be surprised by them. I wonder if she has a deformed leg in her dreams. But how can I possibly ask her this question. She does not like her deformed leg to be touched except at the height of passion, when she instructs me to hold it. I stretch out my hand in supplication. She brushes it aside. I don't care for your attitude, she says. She also succeeds in keeping me awake for another hour. It is no wonder that I keep thinking of the small bookstore on the Left Bank. No one disturbs me as I reverently turn the pages of the book with its sumptuous illustrations of the Great Mosque of Kairouan . . . I walk barefoot over the large flagstones of the courtyard. It is after sunset, but the flagstones still retain the heat from the sun.

6

In the presence of Ludmilla's deformity everything recedes in importance. After only three days she has succeeded in distracting me from the color plates, those illustrations that have come to represent my newly acquired grammar. As for that other past, the one where Alicia, with a look of anguish, reigns supreme, the one that does not start or arrive at any configuration remotely resembling the illustrations of the Mosque . . . it is soon to become completely indecipherable. As a result I shall be a richer man. Since it is clearly no longer a question of repressing the past, now that it has ceased to impose its tyranny upon me, the brain—as insatiable as ever—must be redirected toward enlarged dimensions of satisfaction residing within my newly acquired freedom. After all, the illustrations, as I'm the first to admit to Ludmilla, are only a distraction. They allow me to scrutinize my expectations, my ecstatic joys, and my feverish desires in a fresh context.

But obviously, and this is made manifest by Ludmilla's highstrung behavior, my distractions are just so much copper tubing . . . just so many junked radiator caps in Hoboken. She drums her fingers on my left shoulder blade. I wisely abstain from any mention of my singular pastime. The world has come bearing gifts. It will not forsake me simply because I'm alone and unattached. The scent of roses lingers on long after my lips have left the nape of Alicia's neck. Four years later, to be precise. There are a good many straws in the wind to indicate that Ludmilla intends to make use of my visit. Otherwise she would never tolerate my delinquent sexual behavior.

Breakfast
Breakfast
Breakfast
Breakfast
Breakfast
Breakfast
Breakfast takes forever: Without being the least bit self-conscious, Ludmilla hurriedly downs, munches, pulverizes eight slices of toast heaped with marmalade. She also drinks three cups of coffee. Admittedly all this is done out in the open. One must concede

her a fundamental honesty for not attempting to hide this uncontrollable hunger, nonetheless, the nutritional value of white toast remains debatable. This morning Ludmilla has black rings under her eyes. She is in a hurry and keeps glancing at her wristwatch. I force myself to adjust to her carniverous appetite. Discreetly she lets me know that my offer to help prepare breakfast is most acceptable. A woman of otherwise fastidious taste, she gets carried away at breakfast, pouring the marmalade straight out of the jar. In some respects the breakfast procedure is a most inefficient one. The toaster is defective. Also it is placed at some distance from the table where we eat. Something about Ludmilla, I do not exactly know what, discourages me from offering her any advice. Unable to supervise the toaster from the table I simply have to be on my toes. It is chiefly a matter of coming to grips with the situation. I can easily breakfast later on. Ludmilla drinks three cups of coffee. Since the perculator makes only two, this entails my having to prepare another pot. Emptying the coffee grounds into the paper bag filled to the brim with yesterday's garbage is probably the most discouraging part of it all. The burnt toast I discard are not the result of my inattention, but caused by the toaster's failure to pop up in time . . . occasionally it pops up too soon, which amounts to the same thing, since I then press it down again.

Under the circumstances, it is hardly surprising that our conversation is a cursory one. She evinces an interest in how I live. My mind is on other matters. I keep burning my fingers. I simply have no aptitude for organization. My timing is all wrong.

Don't worry, she says not unkindly. You'll soon get the hang of it.

I am flabby and shifty-eyed. Is it any wonder that hatred frequently holds me in its relentless grip. What am I to make of my rather ill-defined role in this apartment. Ludmilla has stocked up on Medaglia d'Oro and English marmalade. If I'm to stay another ten days, I will see what I can do to add some strawberry jam to the larder.

Now the apartment is empty. No trace of Victor. His name is not listed in the Manhattan directory, or in her address books. I have been letting my brain run rampant. Above all there's that baffling fear of loose and shifting floorboards.

7

A brief rundown of Ludmilla's outstanding features cannot fail to disquiet me further. Her pale finely boned face, at dusk or in poorly lit rooms, bears the unmistakable quality of a Pre-Raphaelite painting. Only an admirer of the Renaissance could have so lovingly recreated the slightly pointed almost translucent quality of the chin . . . and those myopic blue eyes that she disguises with her piercing stare. She has flawless skin. She is also fragile, with delicate wrists, and possesses one exquisite leg. One perfect unmatched leg . . . As is to be expected, she looks her best when bedecked with lace. Lace heaped over her marvelous tits, draped over her bare flank, and thrown over her crown of blonde hair. Her notable breakfast point: eight delicious slices of toast dripping with marmalade.

Do I have a low creamy voice, she asks.

Will this lipstick do.

Is my skirt too long.

Do you like the shape of my knee . . . and what about the elbow . . . and the pink soles of my feet.

For an assistant curator of costumes, her tastes not only vary, one might say they are excessively eclectic. Her preference is eighteenth-century fornication at the court. A popular ladies' magazine claims that she expertly runs her apartment, runs the airy informality of the air-conditioned interior, runs with a slight limp from bed to bath, oblivious of the open shutters, runs from one formal tableau to the next, from one hairy lover to another . . . ceaselessly, defiantly, spreading her legs, one strong and muscular, the other half its size, against a captivating setting of carpets, damp pillowcases, and Wagner on the record player.

Are you, she worries, sufficiently interested in my nipples.

I avert my eyes.

Her needs menace me like the rows of lace on an Empire dress that is sashed in purple satin. Will she continue to prevaricate, to postpone the final outrage while wearing a strapless evening dress with a tiered skirt cut high in front to reveal a flash of one lovely exposed leg . . . I can see it and its mate entwined around an upholstered chair. I feel bound to warn her that one can push things just so far . . .

I keep being struck by her carniverous reactions. Relentlessly, despite my pleas for mercy, Ludmilla sinks her teeth into the soft part of my shoulder, and into the nape of my neck. Unhurriedly, in the poor light, she inspects other sites as well . . . savagely she bites into my neck. Does this bring back memories of Paris. I dare say it does reawaken something, but my memory regarding her is short. I had the foresight to dismiss and forget most, if not all the details of her brief stay in my room. With a certain degree of luck, the subject need never again crowd my brain, once I return to Paris. I shall simply have to guard myself against any impulse to trace the long livid scratch on my back to its origin . . . All the same, her teeth implant a familiar resurgence of terror that I had not thought myself capable of feeling. Ah, where are those beautiful days of roses.

Must you figure everything out in advance, she asks me.

Now she's on edge. She's determined to keep me awake, while she helplessly, almost against her will, subjects me to a seemingly endless account of my room in Paris. I explain that I no longer live there . . . as she well knows, I have since moved to another place without the least bit of regret. But as far as she's concerned, that room has lost none of its former pervasive significance for her. She catalogues the interior, methodically, with an eye to those details that I have overlooked, or admittedly never noticed. It is depressing to hear her speak so lovingly of the louvered shutters that were painted white on the inside . . . and of the tiny bathroom, where in place of a tub stood a bidet . . . and the ancient gramophone left by a former tenant . . . and the photograph of the crouching woman. Yes, the photograph seems to have become a most significant landmark for her. It is over two years since she's seen it, but she remembers it vividly. Now in the soft light of the bedroom lamp, sitting upright on the bed, hugging her legs and resting her chin on her knees, she compels me . . . she forces me to disclaim the accuracy of her account.

Ludmilla insists that she can recall standing mesmerized in front of the mirror that hung in the alcove of my former room . . . so taken was she by the photograph of the crouching woman that I had, on a moment's whim, stuck into the ornate gilded frame.

Don't you remember, she asks insistently. Don't you remember. It was a warm day, and I was wearing a sleeveless white dress . . . Looking at the photograph I suddenly felt a chill, and found myself gently caressing my bare arm. You had run down to buy cigarettes, and must have been away all of fifteen minutes, during which time I remained rooted to the spot, quite shattered by the discovery of the photograph . . . I hadn't spotted it earlier. I must have been sitting with my back to it. I turned just as you were leaving, and my exclamation of surprise must have been audible to you on the landing outside . . .

In this, for all I know, she may be right.

Have you put it up in your new place, she asks me gravely. She also tries unsuccessfully to emulate the expression of fear on the woman's face.

Who was she?

The woman . . . I don't know.

Ludmilla has a tendency to overreach herself . . . excitedly, in her usual flamboyantly high-strung manner she continues: how can this photograph fail to inflame a man . . . seeing a woman crouching . . . utterly defenseless . . . submitting herself like this . . . Ludmilla balances herself unsteadily on the bed. Undoubtedly she is correct. Ahh, where are those beautiful, sanctified days of roses . . . But hair can act as a dense deterrent. The unmistakable stubbles of hair that crown her nipples severely handicap me. One is not the same for the remainder of the coitus . . . Hair has its place, but not in the mind.

Late at night a door bangs shut. It's all right, she says. It's only Victor leaving. I cannot account for my distress. Love does not have the resolute perfection of the courtyard of the Great Mosque of Kairouan.

NOW LUDMILLA OPENS HER WIDE MOUTH AGAIN.

9

To Ludmilla's annoyance I don't seem to recollect why Alicia and I separated. Have you blocked it from your mind?

Oh, nothing of the sort. I just can't recall what sparked it off. We never discussed it . . . not face to face, at any rate . . . It was agreed upon that I would go to France. I just had a bad spell of breaking things. The move was largely a self-protective one. We decided to sleep in separate beds. Alica felt apprehensive that I might hurt myself. Believe me, the bond that united us was more than her father's money. It was her white skin, and the nape of her neck . . . also the way she would sit for hours on end combing her long hair. Her languid pose kept reminding me of a painting by Titian . . .

Ludmilla catches me looking at her misshapen leg, and bluntly asks: What is it? I automatically reach up to draw the blinds . . . But there are no blinds in this apartment. Her tongue completely fills my mouth. I take a deep breath, and then another . . .

. . . what insurmountable difficulties must have faced the architects of that fantastic Mosque . . . Alone the difficulties that had to be overcome transporting the immense marble pillars . . . I can see the caravans coming from afar, loaded down with the polychrome tiles, with the stones, and with the capitals for the Great Mosque of Kairouan. My never having been to North Africa does not prevent me from familiarizing myself with the Mosque's sun-drenched courtyard . . . or with the row of pillars that are joined together by tie-braces at the top, and the ancient inscription, both in Arabic and Latin, on the massive blocks of stone, many of which were salvaged from palaces, fortifications, and basilicas in Italy and Spain . . . I now can clearly see the egg-white ribbed dome, the cobalt blue frames of the crosshatched windows, and the gleaming white walls . . .

Ludmilla mumbles in her sleep, then, quite distinctly, says: Darling. But is she speaking to me or to someone else. I make an inventory of all the details I have overlooked on previous occasions as I pass from one section of the Mosque to another. After only one perusal of the book I can accurately describe the illustrations showing the row of classical columns lining the arcades on the east and west, but not the columns lining the nineteen naves of the sanctuary. The eye is so tremendously selective. The exterior of the Mosque is covered with many layers of whitewash, and when viewed from below, the walls stand out in sharp contrast to the Mediterranean sky above.

Unlike most passionate involvements with the past, illustrations, it seems to me, are not necessarily regressive. I find this reassuring. I have no wish to be imprisoned in a Parthenon of rosy memories. The illustrations merely reflect my almost incomprehensible search for a love I have never felt. Ludmilla groans in her sleep. To whom is she speaking in her dreams?

10

Breakfast
Breakfast
Breakfast
Breakfast
Breakfast
Breakfast

Breakfast takes forever: Anger makes Ludmilla so much more attractive. She is spoiling for a fight. I pinion her arms behind her back. Although it is quite late, she offers no resistance. She grits her teeth, all the while staring at herself in the mirror.

Now, she says through clenched teeth. This word "now" strikes me as odd. I inspect myself in the mirror. Of course I am not blind to the intensity of her feeling. The word "now" has incapacitated me. When is NOW? I dread its passing. Now everything is beyond my grasp . . . One must sustain and crowd each NOW with all one's valuables . . . with all the objects in the apartment, until there's no room left to contemplate its passing . . .

Ludmilla steps into the bathroom. Quickly, with bold efficiency she applies the lipstick. I observe that she fails to wash . . . she also neglects to put on a pair of panties. After she has left I discover evidence of our recent bout staining the floor. Later I shall study the floor of the elevator for further evidence of her irresistible charms. I remain dazed by the evanescent NOW. The NOW in my mind has no future. I return to her desk and look at her appointment book. She has put my departure down for seven P.M. In the desk drawer I find a letter from my wife to Ludmilla. You like to see yourself as a woman in chains, Alicia wrote . . . I recognize countless trite novels and even films in your every move and gesture . . . I even have come to see the contrived obsessional fantasies of my husband in your highly charged conduct . . . as well as in the situations that you exploit. In that respect, even he, poor devil, did not get off without paying a small price for his two weeks with you in Paris. I never suspected at the time that when you asked for his address you actually intended to look him up. You must concede that I've always been obedient and uncritical of you and Frank.

How readily I permitted myself to be recruited as a witness for your bizarre involvements. You had only to threaten me with the loss of my freedom to make me comply. Now I discover that your freedom consists of being a prisoner. When you were staying with me, I kept repeatedly asking myself: Is this what they did in Paris? Is she emulating him. Your ensuing affair with Victor and Frank was more than I could bear. Subtly you attempted to poison our minds, until one of us would turn against you, and in a fit of anger, inflict upon you all the tortures you desired. You made me despise you since that was preferable and less harmful to loving you. Your deep and profound distrust of love made you invite my husband to stay with you. His equivocal attitude toward women, his potential cruelty and violence gave you a temporary feeling of satisfaction. I know the word "sadist" is a delightfully provocative word for you. But he's not a sadist. He's quite insane, and had he stayed with me one day longer than he did, I would have had him committed to an asylum. He fled for his life, just as I now flee for mine.

Among Ludmilla's books is one that I gave her two years ago. I remember the occasion. We were standing arm in arm in the Tuileries. The roses were in bloom. Ludmilla was laughing. The familiar handwriting, the unmistakable handwriting on the title page of the book I had given her fills me with a profound melancholy. TO LUDMILLA WITH INTENSE LOVE AND ADMIRATION. I had neglected to put down the date. Why do the two lines of the letter V disturb me . . . why does the letter L fill me with self-loathing . . . I can read my despicable self-revealing dependency on the distractions provided by the illustrations of mosques in the letter O. Can I never escape my handwriting. Will the letter E pursue me to the bitter end. Now I seek to detach myself from it.

11

As far as I can recollect, it is the third window from the left. When the bamboo blinds are raised it is possible to see a section of the paneled wall of mirrors. The sumptuously outfitted bathroom is situated on the second floor as well. But its windows face west, and are therefore not visible from the garden. It is a hot and humid day. I approach Alicia's house with circumspection . . . I walk quickly, hoping not to be observed.

The letter to Ludmilla no longer rankles. Will you show me

your singular lack of surprise . . . Alicia, will you offer me your cool cheek to kiss. It's no use resisting. I shall have to tie your hands and gag you, because your dreams of delirium might distract me . . . I will make you crouch on the floor and return the look of anguish to your pale face. How will you explain this situation to Ludmilla? I observe shudder after shudder run down your spine. Now . . . I hold my wrists under the cold water faucet. How irresistible your inertia . . . your total lack of resistance. I ask so little of you. Once again, bravely, you look straight into my eyes.

You are not in the kitchen. You are not in the vestibule, 8 by 3; or in the hall, 6 by 9; or in the living room, 11.6 by 14; or in the dining room, 21 by 17; or in the partly dismantled library, 15 by 19.6; or in any of the closets . . . I climb the stairs . . . and tap gently on the door of the bedroom. Overcoming my revulsion I push open the door. It swings back . . . I exercise a certain restraint to keep myself from hurling obscenities at the pale grey ceiling. The sun is streaming through the windows . . . Alicia permitted me to resuscitate my childhood in this room. Now I have come to say good-by. As a child, I remember liking the way the square panels of mirrors formed a grid over everything they reflected. I permitted those 6-inch squares to dissect my desires . . . They continue to haunt me to this day. I thought I had freed myself, but I had simply substituted the large flagstones in the courtyard of the Great Mosque of Kairouan for the paneled mirrors of my childhood.

. . . the bamboo blind can be lowered with a swift whirring sound, a rasping noise similar to that created when a piece of paper is torn out of a spiral notebook, or when that paper, for instance, is lodged inside the protective wire cage that covers the rotating blades of a small table-model electric fan . . .

The thick-set man is wearing a pin stripe suit. I can see him clearly. He is standing close to my mother. The bamboo blind is raised. The man has just entered the room, and in his customary way embraced the young boy. It is eight in the evening. It must be Saturday or Sunday on account of my being permitted to stay up so late. Downstairs the table has been laid for eight . . . but the guests have not yet arrived. If not for the noticeable coolness of my mother, the man, most likely, would already have left the room. True, she permits him to kiss her on the cheek. Something the man, now standing restlessly at her side, said earlier may explain her irritation with him. After all these years I can no longer remember what it was . . . besides, if I did hear it, I may not have fully understood its significance. It is quite possible that her anger is due to his returning home so late . . .

The man speaks to her in his soft and gentle voice, but she refuses to be appeased. The man plays with the cords of the blind, accidentally releasing it, instantly blocking both their views of the garden. It is exactly at this moment that the piece of paper is inadvertantly lodged in the electric fan. The sound must be quite audible . . . but they do not turn around to look at the culprit. To the boy it sounds as if the bamboo blind was being lowered and lowered and lowered in one continuous motion. Apologetically the man raises the blind. Timidly he addresses her again. This time she deigns to reply, but her low voice is inaudible to me. After an initial hesitation the man then places his square and stubby fingers on her soft arm. One endures the pain of being betrayed without appealing to anyone for help. One also suffers from a feeling of suffocation. They both speak in a low voice in order not to be overheard. Now his hand rests on her bare arm. She remains immobile and makes no attempt to withdraw her hand. Now the square fingers of the man, so different from the boy's long and tapered ones, are kneading her soft and pale skin, of which she is so justifiably proud. Doesn't she consider the man's touch objectionable. Certainly nothing on her face indicates any awareness of the impropriety of the man's gesture. In point of fact they continue their conversation as if nothing out of the ordinary has taken place. The man continues to squeeze her arm and she even manages to smile . . . Downstairs the doorbell rings. Just before leaving the room, she looks distractedly at the boy, as if seeing him for the first time. The man winks conspiratorially, and then in an unusual gesture kisses the boy, who, as soon as they have left the room, turns off the fan and immerses himself in the task of extricating the piece of paper that was accidentally lodged between the blades of the fan.

The blind can be lowered with a whirring sound, instantly cutting off the view of the pale grey ceiling and a section of the paneled wall of mirrors as well as the disembodied slim arm
COLOR: WHITE
with the gold filigree bracelet, that is gripping the cord of the blind. At times one can catch a glimpse of a shoulder . . . but I can no

longer tell if the sound of the descending bamboo blind reaches
to the far end of the formal garden, so different from this one . . .
I continue to press my search for you in the bedroom, 18 by 21;
in the closets, those spacious closets . . . I must put my thoughts
in order.

Alicia has left in a hurry. In her letter she mentioned her fear,
but it was not fear that drove her away, it was caprice . . . By
comparison with Ludmilla she is a neat person . . . everything that
was left behind in her drawers is neatly folded . . . I am soon
enveloped by the scent of roses. The unforgettable fragrance brings
tears to my eyes. I leave thumb marks all over the polished brass
doorknob.

12

Have you packed yet, Ludmilla asks me when I return to the apartment. But I'm not due to leave for another three days . . . Victor
is nowhere to be seen. I have a poor memory. I am exceedingly
forgetful, and no longer remember the precise wording of Ludmilla's invitation. I now think it possible that I read something
into the invitation that was not there. Was I brought over to tor-
ment Alicia? At night, following my visit to Alicia's house, my
former home, I lie in bed listening to Ludmilla's trenchant observations regarding her lost youth. She still carefully nurtures the
illusion that she is frail and helpless. She lovingly retouches the
portrait she paints of herself in the Brooklyn Botanical Garden with
the essays of Emerson and the works of Henry James as her sole
nourishment. Strange, I keep seeing Stekel's name on the cover
of the book she is carrying. A peripatetic philosopher, for whom
Aristotle was in no time replaced by Wittgenstein. Now she describes the white dresses she wore as she toured the rose garden.
I can hear someone in the next room. It must be Victor.

Ludmilla's calendar of love has always excluded me. She and
my former wife have always seen to it that I remain the outcast.
Ludmilla seeks uncomplicated affairs. She is drawn to blond mus-
taches and men like Victor. What makes me so boiling mad, says
Ludmilla in her tough and bitchy voice, is your complete disregard
of other people's privacy. How dare you trespass . . . Just because
you idolized my breasts gives you no right to search my belongings.

You will never give me as much pleasure as Victor does . . . why . . . Ludmilla points an indelicate finger at me . . . you require the illustrations of a mosque to support your crippled fantasy.

I think it is her anger that I find so irresistibly exciting. Also the way she crosses her good leg over her misshapen one. Sitting beside her, I tentatively extend one hand, placing it over her bare thigh. I'm certainly not contemplating another joust. Ludmilla does nothing to hinder me. On the contrary, she moves her midriff suggestively, shamelessly exposing herself, if I read her motions correctly, to facilitate my bold and totally unrehearsed exploration. Those blue eyes that now stare unseeingly at the antique map that I gave her two years ago as a memento of our brief stay together, have on prior occasions followed an untold number of spectacles between Victor, Frank, and Alicia. I too, I laughingly tell myself, have my finger firmly pressed on the pulsebeat of time.

. . . from where I now stand, her eyes are almost in a straight line with the doorknob. My bare feet rest on the floor some eighteen inches apart. Ludmilla hisses. One of her earrings has fallen to the floor. Poor Ludmilla, no amount of loving will replace your deformed leg . . . Now Ludmilla and I contemplate her other leg. Our heads are bent in silent adoration. Temporarily united, we breathe in and out in unison.

We hold the leg in a strong grip . . . we will not release it. I have never felt closer to Ludmilla. Again I am filled with a passionate love for her. I think I now know why I was so happy when I met her. I thought we might cross the great desert together. I pretended, with her assistance, to decipher my recent past in her eyes . . . a past that excluded Alicia, and the now vacant house. All that time Ludmilla knew that her shriveled leg had wormed its deathlike way into the labyrinth of my mind. Now that you know what death is, the leg seemed to say, you will never cease to respect me. I, the second leg, am the antithesis of all your hopes. Embrace me to your heart.

A STAKE IN WITCHES

PART ONE

My life is straight out of a picture book. I teach a course in economics during the day, and with alarming regularity dream of
taking giant steps at night in order to shake the ineffable witch
who keeps dogging my footsteps. If only I could learn to shield
myself against her denunciations. Oh, for God's sake, Victoria
complains when I mention the witch. Isn't it about time that you
grew up? Must I resort to deception in order to maintain the
picture-book serenity of our life. I call up my parents in Arizona
and inform them about my promotion to assistant professor. I also
mention that we now own two cars, an achievement bound to
please my father.

I still miss the lush green mountains where Victoria and I stayed
this summer. Victoria, acting entirely on impulse, had hired
Octavio to be our guide for the duration of our stay in Mexico,
although she now, somewhat to my surprise, vehemently denies
this. No, she says, it was your bloody idea. At any rate, Octavio,
when we hired him, did not speak a word of English. I did not
consider this an impediment, since it would compel us to work
harder on our Spanish. It was high up in the mountains that I,
for the first time, extinguished a lighted cigarette by firmly pressing it against my forearm. At the time I did this it seemed the
most logical thing to do. Victoria promptly spotted the burn on

my hand, and questioned me about it. It's just a burn, I said happily. The second time, for no discernible reason, I took a cigarette Octavio was smoking and pressed it firmly against my hand. For a day or two afterward Octavio seemed curiously subdued. What's got into him, Victoria asked suspiciously. . . At night I wanted to make love to her, but Octavio was always underfoot.

Victoria still looks in on me whenever I'm in my study. She inquires sweetly if I would like some coffee. Yesterday afternoon I stood up and embraced her. Ever since we returned to the city I've wanted to make love to her. I covered her smooth oval face with kisses . . . but the sound of Octavio sweeping the floor in the adjacent room unnerved me. Poor Octavio . . . he wants to make himself useful.

Get rid of him, says Victoria.

How can I, I ask her. We've brought him over, and now we're responsible for him. Besides, there's no one else here with whom I can converse in Spanish. Victoria is quick to see the humorous side of it. An hour later she says that she feels tired and goes to bed. In the evening she listlessly picks at the food Octavio brought her on a tray. I wink conspiratorially at him when the two of us are alone.

PART TWO

I have just turned thirty. At fourteen I had for the first time heard Tchaikovsky's piano concerto, but it was not until recently that Tchaikovsky made an impact upon me. Now that Victoria has gone I can play music to my heart's content. There's no one to stop me from playing all night. I turn up the volume until the reverberations of the music rattles the china in the cupboard. Octavio who is attending vocational school in Rochester drops by each weekend. He has never heard of Petr Ilich Tchaikovsky, and with a baffled look on his face stares at the two-by-four-foot photograph that is now hanging above the desk in my study. Octavio believes that it is the face of Lenin, an impression that I do nothing to correct. In general he believes everything I tell him. For instance, he believes, all evidence to the contrary notwithstanding, that Victoria is visiting with her mother in South Carolina. The one marked change in Octavio is that he no longer offers to clean up or help with the cooking, and when I address him in Spanish he invariably replies in English.

A day or two at the most was all it took me to accustom myself to Victoria's absence. Of course I still love her with undiminished passion. Yes, the door will always be open to her. She can return any time she wishes without fear of being questioned about her sudden precipitous flight. I realize that the deafening sound of Tchaikovsky may be something of an obstacle, but I prefer to cross one hurdle at a time. Friday evening Octavio found me in my armchair with a blood-stained towel pressed to the side of my face. What happened to your face, Octavio at once asked. Nothing much, I replied reassuringly. I just slipped while I was on the phone, and in falling broke the window next to my desk. Octavio looked unconvinced until I led him into the study and showed him the broken windowpane. He advised me to see a doctor, but I told him that I had already taken two aspirins and felt no pain. You are a real man, Octavio said. I could not help but take pleasure in Octavio's spontaneous and unsolicited admiration. Of course Victoria was upset. I had been speaking to her on the phone. I can no longer remember our exact conversation. She had said something to the effect that she would like to come by and pick up a few of her things. Anytime, I said. Don't even bother to call. The door's unlocked. It was then that I suddenly lost my equilibrium. She must have heard the sound of the cracking glass. It was quite audible. Hello! Hello! She screamed into the phone. Are you all right? But I couldn't speak with my mouth full of glass. Fortunately the cuts I sustained are superficial. You were lucky not to lose an eye, said Octavio. His English is improving, and he now has a girl friend. Proudly he brings her over the next time he comes to see me. Octavio, the girl and I spend a pleasant evening watching television. With glazed eyes I stare at the four-inch screen without comprehending any part of the program that is being shown. I have come to identify myself more and more with Tchaikovsky, notwithstanding the latter's unforgivable anti-Semitism and most questionable sexual idiosyncrasies.

Slight altercation with the wife, eh? says one of my colleagues when he sees the scars on my cheek. Who does he think he is. Slight altercation with the wife. I feel unnerved by his grin, but also somewhat relieved that the news of Victoria's departure has not yet become public knowledge. How oppressive the air is in the city. I think of the green forests and mountains, of the shimmering clear brooks, and of our joyful and unrestrained laughter last summer. I stare broodingly into the bathroom mirror and think that I now can color the picture book in various shades of red. But at least, for the time being, I'm free of the witch. . . I can again open the broom closet without experiencing any dread.

PART THREE

Victoria comes by unexpectedly to pick up a few of her things. She pointedly avoids looking at my face. Otherwise our meeting is devoid of the awkwardness I had expected to develop. She inquires after Octavio. Do you have a boy friend, I ask. She says yes. He is six foot two, and a student at Columbia, where he's involved in radical politics. All this couldn't be further removed from my own rather uneventful existence. I have been working steadily on a paper for a journal of economics, and my back aches. I have trouble at night falling asleep. I listen to the 1812 Overture over and over again, until the neighbors phone the police.

PART FOUR

The dean of the business school slaps me affectionately on the back, and promises to stick by me no matter what. I laughingly declare that excessive passion can be sticky. Obviously we are speaking at cross-purposes. Octavio's girl friend comes to visit me in the afternoon. I have just listened to Tchaikovsky's Fourth, and exuberantly pick her up and swing her around and around in the living room. She is much lighter than Victoria. We end by making love to the music of Tchaikovsky. Finally someone who does not object to the music. I leave the door open to the studio and stare intensely at the photograph of Tchaikovsky. I discover a scar on her back, but cannot bring myself to question her about it. At last, I tell myself, someone who does not get upset when I refer to the witch, who again is dogging my steps. Who is she, Octavio's girl friend asks. Ah, if I only knew.

The next day another telephone call. I have hardly recovered from the first. These diabolical reversions . . . as soon as I hear

Victoria's soft and hesitant voice everything turns black. One day I fully intend to rip the telephone wire out of the wall. It is the only possible defense against this obscene harassment. While speaking to Victoria, I leaned forward to pick up a cigarette, only to find myself plunging headfirst through the air, the ground shooting away from under me. This time I crashed through the other windowpane, the one that was still intact. Perhaps I need glasses to correct my faulty vision. Victoria on the other end of the line could not possibly explain my wild uncontrollable fit of laughter. What's happened, Victoria screamed. These student radicals, always afraid that something has happened. I test a jagged piece of glass with my wrist. My head and shoulders are clearly outlined in the broken window. I seem to live in a world of glass. In testing the jagged edge of glass I inadvertently sever the artery. Whichever way I turn there is glass, but one cannot live in fear of breaking things all one's life. My dear outlines . . . I fumble for the receiver. She has hung up. In the next hour I lose several pints of blood. Unsuccessfully I tie a tourniquet around my arm. No one is at home in my neighbor's house. I'll die like a dog at Victoria's door, only her door is too far away. I'd never reach it alive. Consider yourself a lucky man, says the doctor at the hospital. I mention Tchaikovsky, and instantly there's a rapport between us. Victoria refuses to visit me. When the doctor speaks to her, she urges him to hold me for additional examinations. What kind of examinations, I ask him. He solemnly taps his forehead, and nods sympathetically when I tell him about Victoria. Later in the day I receive a call from my father in Arizona. He's heard the news from Victoria. Of course she hasn't left me, I tell him. We just had a tiff. Don't listen to a word she says. He asks me if I'm in any pain. How's Mother, I inquire. Worried, he says, and then characteristically changes the subject to talk about an outing they had taken. But you believe everything I say, don't you, I ask. You believe your son?

Sure I do, my father replies in an unconvincing voice.

Well then, relax . . . I tripped on our carpet and cut myself on a pair of garden shears Victoria had carelessly left on the floor. When my father fails to respond, I tell him that inside of one year I will receive a promotion to full professor. I'll still make you proud of me.

We are proud of you, my father says politely.

Not enough, I firmly reply. I intend to make you even more proud of me. I like to hear my father's hearty laugh. The hearty laugh has always been his strongest card. Customers trust his laugh. A man who can laugh like that has the world at his feet, says my mother. They're short of beds in the hospital and somewhat reluctantly let me go. Before going home I drop in on my neighbors for a cup of tea, but I must have seriously overestimated my strength, for I promptly faint on their living room floor. They half carry me to my place, and then, after putting me to bed, clear up the broken glass as well as the broken dishes that litter the apartment. Later that night I try to reach Victoria and tell her what a bitch she is, but her phone is busy. At night the stitches in my arm throb unbearably. The intern who put them in struck me as being quite inept. When I remove the bandage I notice fresh signs of bleeding. Some of the stitches are loose, and it requires almost no effort to pull them out. I stagger over to the phone and call the hospital, leaving a trail of blood for Victoria to see when she comes to pick up her belongings. Anyone, I maintain, can spill blood for a cause, but few seem to understand the underlying metaphysical need that determines a test of physical courage. This time, upon my arrival at the hospital, I find the doctor less inclined to discuss Tchaikovsky. Morosely he inspects my wrist. Despite my protestation a nurse administers a sedative. I don't believe in taking anything stronger than aspirin, I tell the doctor. Aspirin will work wonders. Perhaps we ought to place him in a straitjacket, the doctor says with a look of comic disbelief. At night I again dream of taking giant steps forward. I can cover immense distances with no effort at all. I can also hear the cooing sound my mother makes as she tosses a little red ball to me as we play on the front lawn of our split-level ranch house under the bright Arizona sun. I am so tall that I can hardly make out my feet . . . the trouble with not knowing where I stand is that it creates tiny waves of tension in the back of my head. God only knows upon whom I might be stepping now. To my dismay the doctor is still ill tempered the next day, and quite implacable in his refusal to sign my discharge until someone comes to the hospital to pick me up. You're wasting your time, I tell him. My parents are in Arizona, and my wife is preparing for the next student assault on Columbia University. With a look of resignation he signs the necessary paper. Outside it's a beautiful day in April. The sun is shining, and young women, here and there, are crossing the street, their faces alive with the expectation of love. Halfway down the block I begin to feel so weak from the loss of blood that I have to sit down on the pavement. After a short rest I walk to a telephone booth at the next corner. The dean comes on the phone when I call his office and solicitously asks how I feel. A bit tired, I reluctantly admit. He at once urges me to take a few days off. His cheerful buoyant voice instantly revives me. I call my parents in Arizona. How would you like a visitor for a few days? My mother is overjoyed. Life again is full of promise. I hail a taxi and drive back to my place. Inside the house I carefully make my way between the broken pieces of cups and saucers that, quite unaccountably, lie strewn all over the floor. I throw a few things into my valise, and then call Victoria, but no one answers the phone. In the mailbox I find a few bills, letters, and an unsigned note which says: I Love You. All the way to the airport I wonder who the writer of the note might be. Life is a picture-book existence. Down its indescribably narrow corridors we all shuffle helplessly. But so far, I have managed to evade the clutches of women. I keep telling myself that they are all witches. Yes, underneath their radiant faces lies a disconcerting truth.

MORE BY GEORGE

George was too young to have participated in the 2nd Insurrection, although he could vaguely remember the excitement that signaled the end of the fighting. He was five at the time, and only involved in a most peripheral way as a courier. The temporary lull that followed the Insurrection was promptly named the GREAT PEACE by the provisional government.

As soon as the initial euphoria had worn off, the guys in the leather jackets with the bittersweet smiles, who had made the Insurrection possible, were overcome by a restlessness that, at times, would split their battered-looking faces in two. The GREAT PEACE, or the GP as it came to be called, had sapped their confidence, and as a result their sense of defeat contributed greatly to the divisiveness in the country, and finally helped undermine the GP.

At this time, the Military, as usual, contributed its energies, its talents, its massive firepower . . . and above all, its superb intelligence service to the new society. As a result, there was the usual checking into everyone's past and also the inevitable peering into the uncertain future. But the Banks were thriving. People were even opening Bank accounts for their unborn children. With each new account one was entitled to a name selected by a weekly lottery. Some people claimed that the lottery was rigged in favor of the name Mary. As I said before, there are a great many malcontents about, as well as Marys and Toms. Mary from all accounts is a merry person with a sweet disposition. The future seems to have been cut out for her. So why not choose merry Mary? it said on the Chase Manhattan Bank letterhead.

Yet in spite of the GREAT PEACE, those all too familiar moments of quiet terror and of total panic have not abated. But in general, it must be said, the GP is and has been a productive period. People everywhere feel driven to the easel and to the sketchbook. They express their yearning for peace by painting beaming faces. Bright colors are also being used with a certain success. Photomicrography is another popular pastime. But everyone is easily exhausted due to the scarcity of oxygen. Only after years of intensive research was the lack of oxygen traced to the indiscriminate destruction of the South American jungles. In their heyday, the South American jungles had produced sufficient oxygen to meet three quarters of the world's need. When this country purchased the jungles and proceeded to cut them down, no one paid any attention. The paper industry had pushed the idea to begin with. They had maintained that it would prolong the GP by keeping the twelve-year-old typesetters off the streets. Now the jungles are gone. The kids are still in a rut. Most women are called Mary and most men are called Tom.

When Tom and Mary set out for the mountains, they had been living together for almost three years. On their second day out of New York, Tom parked the trailer in a field of buttercups and daisies. Later, Tom stretched out on a cot in the trailer, and from the supine position he observed Mary as she took off her red bikini.

Aren't you tired? Mary asked Tom. He had been driving half the night, but he insisted that he was not, as she rubbed her smooth belly against his face. I wonder if it's the money that's keeping us together, she said in a teasing voice.

Two days later, they picked up George. They had agreed not to pick up any hitchhikers, but they made an exception in George's case. George was six foot two, and so weak and thin that he kept swaying back and forth, like a tall reed in the wind. They hastened to bring him some nourishing food. George told them that he hadn't had a bite to eat in three days. For some reason, George considered this a great achievement. Perhaps this should have put them on their guard, but instead they watched him eat an entire loaf of rye bread and a pound of ham with an expression of quiet satisfaction. When they had picked him up, George had said that he was only going as far as the next town. When they passed through the next town twenty minutes later, George gave no sign of wishing to get off. Two hours later, he was still talking about Ludmilla. Both Tom and Mary went out of their way to be kind to George. They did not interrupt him. They did not even ask: Who is this Ludmilla you are referring to. They kept acting as if everything were normal. As if George weren't in their midst. Sometimes George seemed upset, and the long horizontal scar on his forehead turned a bright red. Mary once asked him about his scar. They were traveling through Georgia at the time. George wasn't at all evasive, at least not in the accepted sense. Once started on the scar, he kept talking without interruption for forty-eight hours. It was one of the most fatiguing experiences that Tom and Mary had to endure during their trip. It also introduced a note of caution into their questions from then on.

Don't you think we should drop George? Tom asked Mary.

They were ensconced in their snug trailer while George, a bit puffy around the eyes from lack of sleep, was at the wheel of their Volvo.

Yes, said Mary. Just make up some spurious excuse why we can't take him any further.

Forthwith? asked Tom.

Mary was beautifully tanned all over except for the part of her body that remained covered by the bikini whenever she stepped out of the trailer. As Tom stood leaning against the tiny sink in their miniature kitchen, he feasted his eyes on the dark triangular area on his wife's body. She in turn focused her somewhat myopic eyes on the firm turgid shape that he kept pointing at her. Thus, for at least another hour, little was said about George, who maintained a steady fifty-five miles an hour, while his eyes, which were the color of his faded blue dungarees, remained glued on the road ahead. As he drove, George kept thinking about Ludmilla. He kept thinking of the snow-capped mountains, of the race, of the explosion, of everything that seemed responsible for the scar on his head.

You're a beautiful lover, Mary confided to Tom. It was an extremely hot July afternoon, and they were reclining on the trailer cot. The air conditioner was turned on full blast. Fortunately the shortage of oxygen was not as noticeable in Georgia. Also there were fewer roadblocks than in the East. On Thursday, they reached Vienna, population 3,718, just as the census takers were leaving. The people in Vienna were about to celebrate the anniversary marking the defeat of the Turks, as well as, one hundred fifty years later, the publication of a slim volume of poetry entitled *Rambles of a Viennese Poet,* a book that was promptly outlawed when it first appeared in print. In their zeal and love for Vienna, the townspeople had erected a replica of the Stefan's Turm. It was only one fifth the size of the original, but three times as large as the one in Vienna, Maryland, which had a population of 420.

The day before Tom left New York, his editor at *Vogue* had handed him several American flags. Tom was not surprised to receive them. They were after all traveling into the interior. Tom had Mary sew one of the flags to the back of his shirt. He also kept one small flag in his back pocket. It was furled around a little stick. While they were in Vienna, Tom waved his little flag at every opportunity, except when George was around. For some reason, Tom's flag waving disturbed George. Perhaps it awakened sad memories of his childhood. In any case, Tom was an exceedingly considerate and civilized sort of guy. Not that George would have ever said anything about Tom's flag waving. He simply went into a deep gloom whenever he saw Tom wave his flag. And no wonder, since he could recall watching his parents shooting out of the window, and having to get out of his crib to run messages for the gentle smiling guys in the leather jackets. Of course, this had taken place a considerable time ago.

Have you noticed? said Tom to Mary. George has this thing about the American flag.

But since George was so dependable, courteous, kindhearted, as well as such a capable driver, neither Tom or Mary had the heart to quarrel with him. As a matter of fact, Tom was so happy about the setup that he would have found it difficult to refuse George any request. For instance, had George asked Tom to let him have Mary (although there was no earthly reason why he should resort to such an oblique method), Tom would most likely, taking everything into consideration, have given his approval, and let George have Mary. . .not permanently, of course. No, only for the duration of the trip. But George never asked Tom for anything. He changed the flat tires, cleaned the car, and did most of the driving, remaining seemingly content throughout.

Are you contented sexually, Mary once asked him, whereupon George fell into a deep reverie which nearly cost them their lives. Fortunately, they landed right side up in a pasture full of radio-active cows. The cows were glowing away in the twilight like so many bloated fireflies. Someone had written in large letters the word PEACE on their sides. Once Mary had recovered from the shock of landing in the pasture, she ran to the trailer for her camera. With her slim legs and lovely selfless sort of smile, she was the quintessence of a fashion photographer. Dashing up and down between the somnolent cows, Mary shot an entire roll of film, while Tom stood by, watching her with a scowl.

When they arrived in Vienna, the streets were gaily festooned and the attractive old houses were decorated with brightly colored paper flowers. Tom and Mary were enchanted by the lifestyle, by the atmosphere, and by the cordiality of the townspeople, as well as by the little brass band which played military marches every afternoon at four in the main square.

Each afternoon Tom would attend the band concert. During the intermission, while the musicians were munching their saltsticks, Tom would wave his flag. He did not cease to be amazed by the instantaneous emotional response. People everywhere would stop in their tracks, and looking visibly perturbed, gaze at him in deep wonderment. A few older women hurriedly made the sign of the cross, others, unable to control their tears, rushed away. By and large, there was a general recognition of the flag. . . Most of the people seemed to have seen it somewhere before. But seeing it again dampened their spirits. Not that the town lacked flags. There were flags everywhere. There were flags hanging from the windows, from the gas-lit streetlights, from the ornate metal railing around the main square, and attached to the bright bunting that decorated the municipal building. But without exception, all the flags were red, white, and red, with the Austrian Imperial double-headed eagle set in the center of the white field.

Despite the curious and baffling response to Tom's flag waving, Tom and Mary continued to enjoy themselves. They grew fond of the radio-active whipped cream and the pastries in the local ice-cream parlor. By now, they had resigned themselves to George's disturbing presence. The three of them were staying at the Palace Hotel. It was the best hotel in Vienna. The maids wore dirndles, and the high-ceilinged bedrooms evoked memories of ladies with ornate hairdos wearing silk dresses that reached to the floor. THINK AND SUGGEST read the sign on the wall above their double bed. After some initial difficulty, Tom succeeded in placing a call to *Vogue* magazine, but it proved a disconcerting experience.

It's me, Tom, said Tom.

Oh yes, replied the editor. How are you, Tom? I haven't seen you in ages. It's nice to hear from you. Why don't we get together and have lunch next week?

We're in Vienna, Tom said patiently. Vienna, Georgia. And we've taken some fine shots of their new steeple.

Vienna. I don't recall asking anyone to photograph a steeple, the editor said vaguely.

Their conversation dragged on interminably. We're leaving tomorrow for the mountains, said Tom.

Tom, be sure to call me when you get back. We must have lunch and talk. . .

We're making good progress, Tom assured him. We also have a new driver. Ha ha. His name is George. . .

Well, it sounds good, said the editor glumly. Are you sure you're not calling from New York?

No, replied Tom patiently. We're in Vienna, Georgia.

Well, keep in touch.

I will, said Tom. He was depressed for the remainder of the day. He was still depressed the next morning. Isn't it uncanny he said to Mary, as if the thought had just occurred to him. George has never asked us where we are going. Not a single time.

I dreamt about George last night, said Mary as she threw a couple of tea bags into the boiling water. Her casual remark only compounded Tom's irritation. Why don't you put on your bikini, he said. Are you afraid that George might drop in? she asked in a spiteful voice he did not recognize.

George doesn't mind the driving. As he drives, he keeps daydreaming about Ludmilla. It is always the same daydream. As usual, George finds himself high up in the mountains observing the start of a race. Ludmilla is one of the contestants. She is wearing goggles and a smartly tailored leather jacket with a fur collar. To all appearances she is unafraid. England and France are also represented. The man at George's side embraces Ludmilla, and then George, at a signal from the man, hands her a large bouquet of red roses. She calls George, Frank. The man at George's side calls him Frank as well. The mountain air is bracing. Over the roar of the engines, George hears the man at his side yell: Just wait. . . No matter what, I shall unite this country. . . A second later, Ludmilla's snowmobile explodes, showering the spectators with tiny metal fragments. Grief-stricken, George watches as the firemen approach the still smoldering wreck of the snowmobile. Ludmilla's body is wrapped in a white blanket that is stained with her blood.

I think my real name is Frank, George confessed to Tom and Mary at dinner on their last evening in Vienna.

Oh really, that's nice, said Mary.

Frank what? asked Tom.

I don't know, said George.

Are you quite certain? asked Tom.

Does it really matter? said Mary.

I don't know, replied George helplessly. He remembered waking up in a hospital. The nurse and the doctor at his bedside had smiled. A really nice bunch of people.

Who am I? George had asked them after he had taken stock of his immediate surroundings.

Just a minute, dear, said the nurse. She looked at the folder she was holding. You're George, she finally said.

Thank you, said George.

Why were you in the hospital? Tom wanted to know.

I don't remember.

It was at this precise moment that Mary realized that she was madly in love with George. It must have showed in her eyes, because it made Tom feel insanely jealous. George continued to smile, shyly playing with a button on his faded shirt.

And what do you propose to do once we reach our destination? asked Tom.

You're being hostile again, Mary softly reminded him.

We have nothing in common, shouted Tom. We're all adrift in a vast cloud of radio-active cowshit.

They left Vienna early the next morning. By ten o'clock, when they stopped for a cup of coffee, they had covered two hundred miles. Mary took a few shots of the cozy interior of the diner, just to keep in practice.

Tom was so dispirited that he no longer waved his flag. Instead, he made derogatory remarks about George. Well, then, said Mary. Why don't you get rid of George, if you dislike him so much? But Tom pretended not to hear, and turned his back on her.

Having reached the foothills and started their ascent, George kept staring intently at the passing landscape as if, at any moment, he expected to recognize a familiar-looking field or cluster of trees. He was worn out from driving all night and all day, but he wouldn't let Tom take the wheel. It's your turn now, Mary kept saying. It's your turn to drive. Don't you see he won't let me, said Tom. By now he had become resigned to Mary's love for George. As for Mary. She kept thinking about George. She kept seeing him whenever she closed her eyes, and whenever she opened them. It must be his sweetness I love, she decided. Yes, his inexpressible sweetness as well as his frail-looking six-foot-two body.

Have you got a girlfriend? she asked George as they drove up the steep serpentine incline, the slate-colored overhanging cliffs on the left, and a sheer drop on the right. Sometime during the afternoon, a low-flying helicopter flew past on their right. They could make out the pilot in the cockpit. Tom waved his little flag, but it was evident that his heart was not in it. Something had gone awry. I could do with some feedback, Tom said angrily. But all I get are invitations to hop in the sack. This was not strictly correct, since he had not received an invitation for the past four days. On Thursday, just as they were about to take their after-dinner nap, the trailer suddenly came to a stop. What is it this time, Tom asked petulantly. When he stepped out of the trailer to investigate, he discovered George standing at the side of the road holding his knapsack.

This is where I get off, explained George with a wan smile.

You must be joking.

Mary looked out of the trailer window and then quickly struggled into her bikini. She was prepared to side with George. She was prepared to accompany George. She joined the men in her bikini, just in time to shake hands with George, who apologized for leaving them in the lurch. Her eyes opened wide in disbelief as she watched George cheerfully trudge across an open field. In the distance, she could see the snow-covered peaks of the mountains.

Where's he going? Mary asked. No answer forthcoming, she ran to the car and repeatedly honked the horn. George turned around once and waved. Somehow, she managed to overcome the impulse to join him. They were, after all, in the middle of the most Godforsaken wilderness.

That evening, George ran into three hunters who asked him where he was headed. North, he replied unhesitatingly. After a brief pause, one of the men invited George to join them for a bite to eat. A man in a stained leather vest, the oldest of the group, asked George how come he had a large scar on his forehead. George smiled cheerfully and mentioned having driven nonstop from Vienna, Georgia. I can do with very little food or sleep, he said with a quiet modesty.

Where are you going to sleep tonight? asked the first man.

George rose unsteadily to his feet. I think I'll be on my way. They let him go. Afterward, they mused and puzzled over George's destination. They had shot five men in an altercation in the last twenty-four hours, but the thought of killing George never crossed their minds. He had that sort of an effect on people.

Nice bunch of guys, said George to himself as he left the three men sitting around a fire. He had a stiff climb ahead of him.

Mary couldn't bring herself to speak to Tom. In her heart of hearts, she was still yearning for George. She kept repeating his name to herself. George, George, George. It had such a warm ring to it. After a restless night in their trailer, Tom took the wheel. They drove in absolute silence until they reached the mountain resort where the race was to take place. To their surprise, a large crowd had already assembled. Many of the people present had Nikons with 200 and 300 mm. lenses dangling from shoulder straps slung loosely over one shoulder. Tom and Mary kept spotting a great number of familiar faces. They kept saying, Hi there, to everyone they knew. One reporter whispered something into Mary's ear, and to Tom's extreme annoyance, she burst out laughing. The President and his close friend Frank arrived an hour later. Ludmilla stood beside her snowmobile. Her long hair was tucked into her helmet. She looked at the President, waiting for him to turn toward her. But the President took his time. While speaking to a group of reporters, he pointedly refrained from looking in her direction. Tom would remember her standing next to her machine, biting her thin lips, and holding in one hand the little red book on the cover of which was the picture of Mao, the man who had been so instrumental in shaping her life. . .her persistence. . .her will to win. On a slope nearby, people were standing in line, patiently waiting their turn to enter the outdoor latrines. Everything, but absolutely everything was behind schedule. Tom watched the President embrace Ludmilla. Frank, the President's friend, stood a little to one side, holding a huge bouquet of roses. The starter's signal was followed, a split second later, by a tremendous explosion which knocked most people off their feet. The immense heat of the fire buckled the metal of Ludmilla's snowmobile. The fireball was recorded on film by all the reporters and television crews. Within minutes, the nation was informed of the disaster.

This is no accident, the President somberly told one of the CBS reporters. We have permitted ourselves to become accustomed to the unexpected. All that will now have to change. The unexpected from now on must be anticipated.

Mary was the first to spot George on the highway. It's George, she squealed. Tom pulled up, and George got into the back of the car. He was out of breath. I think I'll take a short nap, he said. Mary, to Tom's annoyance, insisted that he lie down in the trailer. The next morning, George cheerfully offered to spell Tom at the wheel.

Maybe this tragedy will unite us, Tom said to Mary.

Us? She looked genuinely puzzled.

I meant this nation, he said hastily. Why did he detest George so much.

Their car broke down outside Vienna. Rather than wait and have it repaired, Tom sold it to a junk dealer from Denver who happened to be passing through. It gave Tom an excuse to spend a few more days in Vienna. Mary was furious when he told her what he had done. But she felt better when the desk clerk at the Palace Hotel greeted them by name. That night as they were eating their Wiener Schnitzel, Tom spotted the President and his entourage entering the hotel dining room. It's the President, he whispered to Mary and George. As the President was sitting down at a table only a few tables away from theirs, George heard him mention the name Frank. George was so startled that he spilled his mug of beer. While a waiter was mopping up the beer, Tom rose from his seat and waved his flag at the President. The President's friend pointed out Tom to the President, who laughed, and promptly invited Tom and his friends to join him. They sat down at the President's table and watched him eat. They also listened to him as he spoke somberly to Tom and Mary about uniting this country. He also patted George lightly on the knee, and then, in a slightly lowered voice, asked him if he would care to join the Presidential party, since owing to the terrible mishap there was one vacant seat on the helicopter. Showing no surprise whatever, George cheerfully said, yes, and then went upstairs to fetch his knapsack.

The helicopter never made it to Washington. It was shot down over North Carolina. There were a great many malcontents in the nation, and people everywhere were dropping words, such as: "hegemony" and "plurality." In all, there were three fatalities on board the helicopter, but the President pulled through, and so did George. It was the beginning of a lasting friendship.

When George regained consciousness in the hospital, he thought of poor Ludmilla being consumed by a fireball. Poor, poor Ludmilla. Now he would never hold her in his arms.

A pretty young·nurse asked George if he wanted anything.

Yes, he said. I'd like to know who I am.

She left the room, presumably to find out who he was. This gave George a few minutes to think. . .he also tried to touch his scar, and discovered that his forehead was swathed in bandages.

You must be Frank, said the nurse, when she returned to his room.

Thank you, said George. I've suspected it all along. For the time being he felt pretty content. In a matter of days he had made so many friends.

HOW THE COMB GIVES A FRESH
MEANING TO THE HAIR

THE ROADS

Some of the roads of Albuquerque permit the people to view the fine scenery from outside the city. The Pueblo Indians used to build roads that dissolved in the vastness of what lay outside of their experience. With a detachment quite unknown to the late settlers of Albuquerque, the Indians observe the growing Albuquerque network of roads until its grid system finally encompasses "The Brook of the Running Spirit," and splits into two "The Mountain That Is Too Hot to Touch." Now and then a new road will provide a visitor access to a museum. Now and then a road will also launch a new cabbie. . . There are already far too many cabbies stationed in front of the Albuquerque railroad station. There are also far too many cabbies blocking the roads, blocking with their battered vehicles what the Pueblo Indians describe as "The Elsewhereness of Things." The cabbies won't budge until their demands are met. But they suffer from poor leadership. They also suffer from a lack of public sympathy. They are not retarded, at least not according to the prevailing medical standard, and therefore cannot expect to elicit sympathy for their plight.

THE CHILDREN

The retarded children have managed to live through another hot summer. They are now staying among the Indians in a pueblo that is less than an hour's drive from Albuquerque. The terrible events that took place on the blocked roads just outside of Albuquerque have not marred their memories. They have emerged unscathed by the experience. In any event, they are still considered as being sacred by the Indians, who have taught them to make ceremonial masks and weave baskets for the tourist trade. Following the events that have been described in some detail in a voluminous eight-volume work entitled *The Remembrance of Albuquerque*, the children traveled in a Greyhound bus, flew in a helicopter, and on one unforgettable occasion sailed on a yacht on the Potomac. This was on the occasion of their visit to the capital to receive the Medal of Merit for Retarded Children. A memento of their visit is a large wall-sized map of Washington. Back in their small adobe and stone house in the pueblo, the map hangs on the wall of their playroom. They do not yet understand the meaning of the map. The map, in their minds, resembles a sand drawing for a ceremonial Navaho dance. How can they, existing as they do in a state of retardation, distinguish a network of streets from a network of elaborate mythological destinations.

THE COMB

The comb parts the hair and exposes sections of the white scalp underneath. The comb gives a fresh meaning to the hair. It serves as an indicator. It provides a sort of explanation. The comb is made of plastic, but in the children's retarded hands this hard resilient material is kneaded into a softer and more rubbery substance resembling the unparalleled softness of their faces.

NAMES (1)

The retarded children have names. They do not always remember their names. They do not, consequently, always respond to their names. . . They are not even sure what a name is meant to be. They are called: Harry, John, Dwight, Lyndon, Dick, Frank, Bess, Jackie,

Minnie, Lady, Pat, and Eleanor. In themselves the names do not with any specificity indicate the nature of their abnormality. The Pueblo Indians are convinced that their abnormality is sacred, and that everything that is related to the children is equally sacred. The children's names are listed on their medical reports and on their birth certificates. The certificates are stamped: RETARDED. The children and the Pueblo Indians take sacredness for granted.

MRS. DIP

Mrs. Dip arrived in Albuquerque three years ago. Her first name is Clara. Naturally, she visited the Pueblo Indians, and examined their weary faces. She also climbed the tall wood ladders that lead into their ceremonial chambers by herself, quite unafraid, somehow radiating a purity and confidence. It came as no surprise to anyone when the town council by a unanimous vote elected Mrs. Dip to work with the poor retarded children who had been left in the care of the city fathers.

MARRIAGE

Even the retarded children cheered when Mrs. Dip said: I do. They now formed a nuclear family. The ceremony was a simple one. Mrs. Dip walking barefoot down the aisle to be purified by the priest, as the children knelt and the Pueblo Indians in their ceremonial robes danced outside. The event, like so many of the events that are to follow, has been preserved on slides. Mrs. Dip at first failed to understand what the Indians meant when they spoke of the children's sacredness. But she is finding out. . . Shall we have a barbecue tonight, asked Mr. Dip. Yes darling, she answered, thinking, this is the bliss I've always wanted to experience.

GLASS

Mrs. Dip is only twenty-four. Her young shining face is visible through the windshield. The shatterproof windshield increases the distance between her and the retarded children who are clamoring for her attention, for her love, for her unbearably sweet embraces.

They have grown accustomed to being caressed by her. But once inside her car Mrs. Dip is unapproachable. Sadly the children stand on the promontory of the pueblo and watch her drive away in a cloud of dust. It is the sweeping cloud of the spirit, say the Pueblo Indians, consoling the children.

Each day Mrs. Dip drives from a small suburb of Albuquerque to the pueblo. In order to reach the pueblo she drives across a narrow bridge spanning a canyon. She and the few other drivers who have business at the pueblo drive at a snail's pace, because the bridge is old and unsafe. At the other end of the bridge the children are waiting to dribble their saliva on her freshly starched blouse. They are waiting to scrutinize her carefully, to examine her wardrobe, to register every nuance of change, every minute alteration.

FINGERNAILS

Her fingernails are painted a bright red. The bright red shatters the already tense atmosphere of expectation. Mrs. Dip may not be aware of it, but to the children her hands are sending out signals which they are trying very hard to interpret. The reasoning behind this is simple. If they can comprehend what she is saying with her hands, they may, in the future, be able to understand the other more intimate signals of her slim and sweet body. The children, naturally, have spotted her bright red fingernails and become unusually unruly. Mrs. Dip hurriedly enters the small room on her left, and firmly closes the door, locking it on the inside. A hush falls over the children. Mrs. Dip has disappeared from sight. Is she in the peeing room? Is she in the Pueblo Indian room of the running water dance, or has she somehow become invisible? They strain their ears, listening for the sound of running water, and dare they hope, for the sound of something else, the intimate sound, the distant sound of Mrs. Dip's body dissolving.

THE CITY

It is built on a large mirrorlike surface. The streets are polished daily. The people avoid looking at the ground in order not to be blinded by the sun. When Marcel Proust first entered the city he

146

did not know where the center was located. He spoke the language but had great difficulty in making himself understood. There are cracks in the mirrorlike surface, but these are carefully disguised. When Marcel first arrived he was particularly struck by the cleanliness and the silence.

Have you come here to study the Pueblo Indians, he was asked, or do you, instead, wish to write about the retarded children?

MARCEL'S CHILDHOOD

In volume one of his great work of fiction, Marcel Proust described a few intimate details of his childhood. He also described his dependence upon his mother. In general, the people he described spent most of their time in sitting rooms. They frequently spoke about their travels, past and future. They compared different cities, cities he had never seen. Like him, all of them were pale. Like his mother, they were afraid of the harmful rays of the sun. It stood to reason that they too would in time imbue him with their fear. In the sitting room they discussed truth, mythology, and relativity with the disconcerting assuredness of people who are convinced that what they are discussing did not exist. In volume one Marcel as a young boy borrowed books from a lending library. Most of the books were about aristocrats. Somewhat timidly Marcel mimicked their laughter. In the books he so avidly read all the salons of the aristocrats were rectangular in shape just like the sitting rooms of other people, except that the salons of the aristocrats were slightly larger to accommodate the pianos and the huge mirrors.

SLIDES

Mrs. Dip's life has been uneventful. She has not read Proust. Seated in her small compact car, the uneventfulness of her life is a surface which she keeps traversing daily. The landmarks that stand out are all recent ones. Mrs. Dip cherishes the landmarks. Mr. Dip eating his breakfast. Mr. Dip mowing the lawn. Mr. Dip buying a five-hundred-dollar leather armchair. Mrs. Dip rewards the children by showing them slides of her living room. The slides were taken by Mr. Dip. The slides show the five-hundred-dollar armchair from every conceivable angle. There are also slides of the electric lawn mower and of the table set for breakfast. The children may be retarded, but they are quite capable of recognizing the glasses of milk and fried eggs on the table. Their reward, it turns out, is a journey through the vaguely familiar-looking world of Mr. and Mrs. Dip. Breathlessly the children wait for the breakfast shown on the slides to be consumed.

THE BED

Mr. Dip has also taken a few slides of their double king-sized bed. These slides were taken during the hopeful period of his marriage. Seeing the bed, the children begin to squirm in their retarded fashion. The bed is inviting. It is large and spotless. It is the place where Mr. and Mrs. Dip spend the night. The children are well informed. The Pueblo Indians smile tenderly as they hear the children laugh. But the slides of the bed are misleading, since on one or more than one occasion Mr. Dip has informed his wife that she smells of retarded children. Everytime she undresses he can see the children's saliva trickling down between her two firm but small breasts.

THE RECKLESSNESS

Marcel Proust did not hesitate when the recklessness came pounding on his door. Despite the lateness of the hour, he permitted it to enter. There is no truth, no mythology, and only a few books of relative merit. Half groggy with sleep he dressed and left the house. Overcoming his innate shyness, he approached a man on the street and asked him where he might find the members of the upper class. You'll find most of them hunting rats in the basement of the Hotel Marigny.

Where's the hotel?

Any cabbie will take you there, said the man.

As Mr. and Mrs. Dip sat in their living room they could hear the recklessness pounding on the door of their neighbor. I don't like to hunt rats, even if one gets to meet members of the upper class in an informal setting, said Mr. Dip thoughtfully.

THE SILENCE

Marcel may have come here because the people of Albuquerque are well known to be tolerant and exceedingly friendly to strangers. However, odds are that he came here because of the stillness. He arrived at midday and was immediately overcome by the silence. For the first two months he stayed in a small second-class hotel. Then, after visiting several real estate agencies, he bought a three-story brick building in an overwhelmingly lower-middle-class neighborhood. The previous owner of the house had been killed by the local butcher after a petty altercation. It did not really concern Marcel. He never met the man's widow. He only dealt with the real estate agent. Do you remember your childhood? the agent asked Marcel. Vividly, replied Marcel. You are lucky, said the agent. You should cherish those memories.

THE FOOTPRINTS

They belong to Marcel. He takes a walk early in the morning. He leaves footprints. Everyone in Albuquerque is startled by Marcel's footprints because the footprints are so small and, somehow, because they appear to be so insidious . . . their ingratiating and self-effacing outlines negating the otherwise determined stride of his walk. People are convinced that anyone capable of walking furtively yet with such a single-mindedness is clearly headed for the peak of fame.

Welcome back little Marcel, welcome back, cry Marcel's sallow-faced lower-middle-class neighbors, as he returns from his walk, invigorated, and filled with ideas for the next incident in his book.

THE FIRST NAME

This is an introduction to the unreliability of the first name. In this instance the first name is Albertine. It is the name of a young woman in Marcel's eight-volume masterpiece. Day after day people keep ringing Marcel's front doorbell. Enough, he pleads, enough, I've got all the information I can use. But they insist on providing him with the latest about the retarded children, calling them the Rets. It took Marcel days to catch on. The rats, he said wonderingly, you don't say. . . They also bring him news about the cabbies and the whereabouts of the woman he loves. . . The one thing they do not bring him is the love he craves. But Marcel was waiting, and when the bell rang, he easily slipped into a faded silk dressing gown and answered the door.

My name is Albertine, said the woman. It happened to be the correct name. Marcel, as it turned out, was anticipating her arrival. There was a fire burning in his study. He stood aside to let her enter, then rushed back to his study and doused the fire. Only some notes for my book, he said in his self-deprecating way. She wasn't aware of the significance of the event at the time.

ALBERTINE'S FALSEHOOD

I don't wish to leave you, she told Marcel. I like this quaint building, and your quaint neighbors, and all your quaint friends, and I'm dying to hear what you've written about me today.

THE LONGING

The cabbies in Albuquerque long for new streets and for new driving regulations. For Marcel, longing is as familiar as the quilt on his bed. He craves for the company of people who are not instantly recognized by the cabbies. Having been invited by the local RET club to participate in a panel discussion on the merits of starvation in the modern novel, Marcel refers to his hunger. I'm starved for Albertine, he declares, when it is his turn to address the twelve people in the audience, but she's never there when I want her. I have compiled a long list of her lies, infidelities, and deceptions. My longing fills me with gloom, just as I know her death will fill me with dejection. I have decided that she will be trampled to death by a horse in the fifth volume of the English edition. That much has been decided. It will give my longing a long needed respite.

VISITORS

While Marcel was amusing the members of the upper class at a fashionable resort which was only four hours by train from the center of the city, Mr. and Mrs. Dip moved into the house next door. Occasionally, while redecorating their new home, laughter from the garden next door would drift over to where they were working. Generally the laughter had an elegant ring to it. Sure enough, when Mrs. Dip peered out of the front windows she could see a large Bentley parked at the curb. Naturally, the Bentley and the uniformed chauffeur attracted a good deal of attention. People from all over came to stare quietly, without any rancor, at the old Bentley and the uniformed chauffeur. Little Marcel is having another important visitor, some said, taking pride in Marcel, taking pride in their neighborhood. No, someone else said. Marcel is away for the month. But this did not in any way diminish the pride.

THE BENTLEY

To this day the old bullet-proof Bentley is the favorite vehicle of the upper class. They prefer it to the Rolls because it is less ostentatious. They like the smooth ride, the leather upholstery, besides, they also save a hundred and twenty dollars on the grill. In his own inimitable manner. Marcel has tracked down all the people with a Bentley in their garage. He now feels free to call their chauffeurs by their first names. During Marcel's absence, one of his numerous society friends dropped by unannounced. Finding Albertine at home, he, out of courtesy, paid her a brief visit. It was this man's elegant laughter that drifted up to the second floor of the house next door, just as Mrs. Dip was musing over her choice of a wallpaper for the bedroom.

THURSDAY (1)

Marcel had arrived in Albuquerque on a Thursday. The cabs were drawn up outside the railroad station. A solid phalanx of cabs. Only four passengers besides Marcel got off at Albuquerque. As soon as the drivers caught sight of Marcel they broke into a run. Something about his face perhaps. . . He had planned to check his luggage at the station and then enjoy a leisurely walk to the center of the city before proceeding to a hotel, but seeing the angry faces of the cabbies he instructed the porter to put his luggage quickly into the first cab. If someone had told him that the blue sky had suddenly turned the color of lead, Marcel would have believed him.

DOUBTS

Marcel sees Albertine dancing with another woman at the Hotel Marigny. They are laughing. It is a coarse, disagreeable laughter. Marcel almost faints.

THE MAP

The map shows the large sprawling city, its squares and parks, museums and theaters, hotels and taxi stands, all within a thirty-minute drive from the large estates that surround the city. Once Marcel unfolded the map and discovered where he was located in relation to the estates, the future, it seemed to him, seemed more promising. The map also indicated the whereabouts of the small airport, and the garages where the taxi cabs are parked at night. The red circles on the map indicate where the cabbies wait for their fare. . . After nine in the evening, most of the men they pick up wish to be taken to the Albuquerque rat hunt. . . The cabbies can instantly recognize a ratter. By now all the cabbies know Marcel. He is a good tipper. They drive past his house and honk their horns, not knowing that the walls of his room have been sound-proofed.

MR. DIP

Mr. Dip is reading because he has time on his hands. He has time on his hands because he is waiting. He wears a clean suit. Ever since his wife started to work with the retarded children, Mr. Dip has worn a freshly laundered suit each day. Mrs. Dip's salary has helped to cover the large cleaning bill, and maintain the immaculately polished interior of their house. Mr. and Mrs. Dip are not planning to have any children in the near future since they already have twelve retarded ones. Soon Mr. Dip is planning to find a companion for his five-hundred-dollar armchair.

NAMES (2)

The retarded children have names. Most of the time they will acknowledge their names. Sometimes they'll pretend to have more

names than one. Marcel's impromptu visit was just such an occasion. It threw everyone into a great fever, and each one of the
retarded children claimed to have at least one dozen names, thereby hoping to remain at the center of Marcel's attention for the
duration of his stay. Mrs. Dip introduces the children. Without
being aware of it, she has introduced Marcel to the great pathos
of retardation. It is not, however, an unendurable pathos for a
ratter.

RATTING

Some attempts have been made to explain ratting. The rats were
pierced with hatpins or beaten with sticks. The people who attended these hunting parties soon discovered that their everyday
conversations took on a new significance when certain words, such
as: return, rattle, retribution, startle, tar, rather . . . were mentioned.
Was Marcel aware of this when he volunteered to visit the retarded
children.

WHAT ARE THE RETARDED CHILDREN THINKING? (1)

They are thinking that it is soon time for supper. They are also
stimulated by the slides taken by Mr. Dip. In their retarded minds
they are desultorily drifting through the as yet incompletely furnished house of Mr. and Mrs. Dip. In their disturbed minds they
are covering the black smooth leather of the elegant chrome armchair with the imprints of their passionate kisses. They also believe,
not incorrectly, as it would appear, that Mrs. Dip is dressing to give
them pleasure, that she is painting her fingernails and toenails to
bring some brightness into their bleak lives. If only they knew that
the saliva they drooled on Mrs. Dip's blouse was depriving Mr. Dip
of his pleasure, they would in their retarded fashion most likely
intensify their ardor, intensify their passionate embraces . . .

Mr. Dip gazes at the breakfast table and then looks out of the
window at the New Mexico sky, thinking that another beautiful
day is awaiting him at the office.

What are the children thinking? Their thinking can be said to be at a standstill. It is colored by the fingernails of Mrs. Dip. It is colored by her long blonde hair. The children are retarded and are learning to tie their shoelaces. Each day they are taught to use a comb. The comb has become a familiar object for their retarded minds. They have become accustomed to its presence and no longer recoil when it is put into their hands. Somehow the hair keeps growing on their retarded heads. It was hair in the first place that necessitated the invention of the comb. The comb is green with a long handle.

THE LETTER

Marcel is attached to his mother. He writes from a resort hotel. He is suffering from hay fever. He has dislocated his right arm. Who is the strange man in boots who is constantly spying on poor Albertine, he wants to know. He's not a member of the upper class, that's for sure, responds his mother. Does she save my letters, wonders Marcel. So much depends on it . . . so much . . .

NEIGHBORS

Marcel failed to see Mr. and Mrs. Dip move their giant bed, section by section, into the house next door. Marcel is away at a resort hotel, said his mother when Mr. Dip knocked on their door. I'm your new neighbor, explained Mr. Dip. I just wanted to borrow a cup of sugar.

ALBERTINE

Marcel maintains that I conspire against him. He questions me about the man who was seen following me yesterday. In volume six he discovers my secret life. It is a lie. In volume five I am thrown by a horse. Another blatant lie. Marcel feeds on the endless lies he loves to fabricate. He feeds on my presence and then spews out the crap that his friends, the cabbies, read while waiting for their evening fares.

LAUGHTER

Despite the cork-lined walls, Albertine's laughter penetrates his room. Who is she embracing now? Each time she laughs he has a fleeting glimpse of her being thrown by a horse . . .

INTIMACY

Albertine reluctantly joins Marcel in his cork-lined room. She complains that it is too hot and disrobes. Carefully she lies down on his papers that are scattered all over his bed. Tell me Marcel, would you still love me if I was someone else?

You are someone else, replies Marcel. That's why I love you.

THE DOOR

The door is attached to hinges which have been oiled. It swings open noiselessly. It permits Albertine to slip out furtively. There is no truth, there is no mythology, and there's hardly any relativity left in the world. She has by now become accustomed to the distortions in Marcel's notebooks. Still, as she intends to prove, the distortions are open to change. However, Marcel doesn't waste any time on regrets. He doesn't challenge Albertine's not entirely unforeseen departure. He simply invalidates it by chipping away at the stone steps, and in place of the entrance he has a large bay window installed, obliterating all signs of her hasty exit.

THE FENCING LESSON

The count's footman watches as his master gives Albertine a fencing lesson. They have to improvise a bit, because the count has sold his foils. They make do with sticks. The count is extremely watchful because there are one or two valuable vases in the room. Albertine is beside herself with excitement. Later that afternoon they go riding on the count's estate. How easily she has slipped away from Marcel. . . How skillfully she managed to open the front door after oiling the hinges. She will change her name if necessary. Marcel will never find her again.

THE CABBIES

Marcel is the only one who sides with the cabbies after they have announced a wildcat strike. Marcel, for shame, says the count. The cabbies are blocking all the roads leading to the city. They are well organized. They also pose a certain threat to our safety. Their families, furthermore, have gone into the streets. Their loathsome faces are peering into our bedrooms. But nothing will change Marcel's position. In the evening his mother makes egg salad sandwiches and distributes them to the starving cabbies who are lying next to their idle machines.

THURSDAY (2)

No doubt about it, Albuquerque has made a deep impression upon me, said Marcel, but it's time that I change my frame of reference. The Thursday after Albertine's departure he packed his belongings, but when he opened the front door he saw a phalanx of cabs drawn up at both ends of the street. I am a prisoner, Marcel concluded. These people need my support. They won't let me leave.

IMPATIENCE

The silence of the city only intensifies Mrs. Dip's impatience. She can't bear to sit down with a book. She can't bear to remain inside a room for more than ten minutes. She can't bear to hear the laughter from next door knowing that she can't join in. She gets into her small car. She is protected by the windshield as the car hurtles forward. People can see her but they can't spray her with their saliva. She drives down the highway until darkness sets in. Mr. Dip is unaware that she has left the house. He is sitting on his new chair. He is sitting contentedly on his hands, humming to himself. He can't wait for it to be time to go to work again, and for the safety of the office. Yet Mr. Dip is well liked in his neighborhood. He smiles a good deal of the time. People refer to him as the cheerful young man whose wife works with retarded children. Each fresh leather armchair he acquires helps obliterate the threat of retardation. Late into the night he thinks of the perfection of furniture.

THE AIRPORT

Albertine flies over Albuquerque in a single-engine plane. It is her first solo flight. The view from the open cockpit is exhilarating. Somewhere down below Marcel is sitting in his cork-lined room writing about her. He wanted me to be thrown by a horse, but I wasn't. If only he could see her now. Sitting at his desk, engrossed by what he is writing, Marcel doesn't even hear the sound of the explosion that rips the plane apart.

CROSSING FRIENDS

1

I wouldn't be writing this if I hadn't, quite by accident, come across a poem by Kenneth Koch, "The Departure from Hydra." The poem crystallized the painful confusion surrounding my own trip to the Sahara. One passage in particular caught my attention: "For a human situation often leads people to do things they don't desire at all, but they find what they did desire has somehow led them to this situation." The line speaks for itself. It is clear that I did not wish to leave for the desert, yet I did. It is also clear that I did not want to bring Doug and Dewitt together, yet I did.

I can still, in my mind, see Doug the day he and his wife moved into the apartment across from my own. I had been walking my dog, and when I returned I saw Doug standing at the foot of the stairs, waiting for the moving van to arrive. I said hello, and introduced myself. He looked amazingly familiar, and I racked my brains trying to think where we might have met. Only later did I realize that I had seen him on stage in some Off Broadway production a few months before.

Doug and his wife invited me to a party soon after they had moved in. I was astonished to see how much work they had put into their apartment, stripping the walls to the bare brick, painting the floors white, enlarging the living room by ripping down several partitions. Most of the people at the party were from the theater world. I recognized a face or two. Doug's wife kept introducing me as their next-door neighbor. In all, I don't believe I exchanged more than a few words with her. Both she and Doug had their careers. He as an actor and sometime model, and she, the daughter of an insurance executive, successfully ran a small boutique on the Upper East Side. Naturally, they both had excellent taste, and I admired all the changes they had made and were still making in their apartment, although I was left with the feeling that their stay was only a temporary one. Still, they kept improving the place, working on it in their spare time. I would see them infrequently. One day I found Doug standing at a nearby street corner, waiting, he said, for his wife. It was on that occasion that I mentioned that I was seriously thinking of going on a long trip abroad with Dewitt, a close friend of mine. But I didn't say where, and Doug didn't ask. I can still see Doug, looking incredibly young and confident. As usual he was wearing his light brown double-breasted blazer. The slight bulge in his right-hand pocket, I later discovered, was caused by a .38 caliber pistol for which he had a permit. The bulge was inconspicuous . . . I don't believe I ever noticed it. For a while I and my dog stood together with Doug waiting for his wife. He didn't say why he was waiting for her on the street so near our building, and I didn't think it my business to ask. When she didn't show up, I became restless. I finally suggested that we go to my place and have a drink. We could keep an eye out for his wife, and she might join us, but he said that he had promised to meet his wife on the street, and she would be disappointed if he was not waiting for her . . . Perhaps another time then, I said. We parted on that inconclusive note. I had hoped he might come up and see my place, since neither he or his wife had ever set foot in it.

2

As best as I can recall Doug had never expressed any desire to meet my friend Dewitt, although I had a number of times mentioned Dewitt to him. On the other hand, to my great surprise, Dewitt had on one occasion spoken to me about Doug. I no longer remember how or why he had come to mention Doug. By now it is quite immaterial. For all I know I may have been the one to bring up the subject. In which case I wouldn't be surprised if Dewitt had responded by saying that he had seen Doug in some Off Broadway performance. He did, however, I remember, say that he would like to know Doug. To my astonishment he said it almost wistfully, as if ever getting to know Doug was beyond his attainment. His exact words were: I would so much like to know someone like Doug. When I told Dewitt that Doug happened to be my next-door neighbor, he reacted as if I had dropped a bomb. What? You know Doug? What is he like?

I no longer recall all of his questions, most of which I could not answer since the only time I ever ran into Doug was on the stairs when I was either leaving or returning to my place. We sometimes spent a few minutes in conversation. For some reason I could not understand Doug's wife was hostile to me, and her dislike, which she did not trouble to disguise, put a damper on the brief encounters Doug and I had on the stairs. All the same, I promptly remember offering to introduce Dewitt to Doug. I could easily, I assured Dewitt, arrange a meeting on the stairs. Doug thanked me, but to my astonishment said, no . . . no, thank you . . . leaving me with the distinct impression that he didn't wish me to be the one who brought them together. I was flabbergasted by his response. I spent an entire day pondering the meaning of his refusal. Perhaps, I reasoned, Dewitt knew more about Doug than I did. Perhaps Dewitt didn't think that I was the correct person to bring them together.

3

Two weeks later when I met Dewitt for lunch he was carrying a map of the Sahara. I must admit when he unfolded the map I felt a surge of anticipation. His invitation came at the right time. I was quite prepared to drop everything I was doing and accompany him to the desert. I had done some traveling, of course, but never in a desert, and naturally the idea intrigued me.

That afternoon carried away with enthusiasm I rushed to the Public Library and looked at some of the books on the Sahara in order to acquaint myself with the terrain, in order to come to some decision, although quite possibly I had already come to a decision without knowing it. Somewhat to my surprise most of the books

made the arduous trip seem extraordinarily simple and uncomplicated as long as one maintained certain elementary precautions,
as long as one did not panic when bitten by one of the deadly
striped and sand-colored vipers, or lose one's passport and innocu-
lation certificate. Apparently they were incredibly strict about such
things at the border. But then there were the other books in which
the same trip in the same identical desert was made to appear
quite hazardous. According to these books the entire desert was
filled with hidden obstacles and all sorts of dangers. It was enough
to make me reconsider my decision to go, to the extent that I had
reached a decision, or left poor Dewitt with the impression that I
had reached a decision. Still, all in all, when I think back, I
hardly glanced at the books. I didn't have the time. Besides, I
couldn't possibly tell which of these contradictory descriptions
accurately described the trip ahead of me. Mostly I looked at the
beautiful color illustrations. When I saw Dewitt again the next day
I was careful not to let him sense my misgivings, just in case I
changed my mind and decided after all to go along, although with
each passing hour this seemed more and more unlikely to me. Still,
I must admit, to my mind the trip became a kind of challenge.
Was I the sort of person who would prove an ideal companion in
a desert. Was I capable of driving the Land Rover in a sandstorm.
Quite honestly, I had no way of knowing. One is always a bit hesitant about forming an opinion about one's capabilities, one's courage, one's determination.

4

I was immensely pleased when Dewitt asked me to join him on
the trip to the Sahara. Being extremely impulsive I may well have
said something that first moment as we pored over the map, which
led Dewitt to believe that I would accompany him. Even my
friends, when I discussed the trip with them, seemed enthusiastic.
Only later did it occur to me that quite possibly my friends were
simply telling me what I wished to hear all along. Since there
seemed to be no point in further discussing the trip with them, I
did not bring up the subject again. I also stopped answering the
phone for fear that it might be Dewitt. I couldn't bear to admit
that I wasn't able to reach a decision. Outwardly I remained my
serene self. But the desert began to intrude into my day-to-day

activities. I couldn't concentrate on what I was doing. I lost all interest in my friends. Then for eleven consecutive nights I had the same dream. Dewitt and I were crossing the desert on foot without, as far as I could determine, any particular objective in mind. The dreams were quite pleasant really, except that each time we crossed the desert, the monotony of the landscape and the sheer boredom of walking in the soft sand filled me with a kind of leaden feeling. It made life with Dewitt, on these repeated crossings—inasmuch as one lives any sort of life in a dream—interminably protracted. Toward the end of the dream I began to equate him with the desert, and for all I knew I was crossing Dewitt while crossing the desert, both the desert and Dewitt becoming the target of my quite irrational anger. I expect the dreams in part were responsible for my decision not to go, but when I finally made up my mind to call Dewitt, he had already left.

5

For no other reason than to clear my mind I started to write about my friendship and affection for Dewitt. I tentatively toyed with the idea of putting my feelings on paper as soon as Dewitt had left for the Sahara without me. I believe that by putting it all on paper I simply wished to clear up a misunderstanding I may have caused by leaving Dewitt with the impression that I would accompany him to the Sahara. At the time of his departure I sat down at my typewriter just as I assume Kenneth Koch sat down at his typewriter to write about the island of Hydra. Koch, as if aware that he is addressing me, writes as follows: ". . . instead of despairing and giving all thought of pleasure up, I felt that if I could write down all that I felt as I came walking there, that that would be a pleasure also. . . ."

Dewitt, I know, has come into a lot of money, and now spends a good deal of his time abroad. Therefore, it is quite conceivable that he and Koch might have met on the island of Hydra, or on some other island, and that consequently Dewitt, farfetched as it may sound, is actually depicted in Koch's poem. I might add that this likelihood does not make the poem more or less meaningful to me. It simply is a possibility, and I record it as such. After all, Koch's poem is not about Dewitt, or for that matter about Doug . . . the poem simply registers the lively expectation one might well expect to find in Dewitt as he plans his next day's trip, or in Doug as he accepts my unexpected invitation to travel to the desert . . .

I would have liked to ask Dewitt if he had ever been to Hydra, and whether he is at all familiar with Koch's poem, "The Departure from Hydra," because, it occurs to me, he too if he read it might discern the faint glimmer of light the poem seems to shed on the tenuousness of our relationship.

6

When I saw Doug standing at the street corner waiting for his young and beautiful wife, I was struck by the look on his face, a look that seemed to imply, to me at least, a complete ease with himself and with the world, a feeling of self-confidence I seem sadly to lack. Sometime later, when I somewhat impetuously invited him to accompany me to the desert, I did so thinking that in some way his self-confidence might make up for my own lack of it. Yes, said Doug thoughtfully, when I rashly broached the trip to him, the Sahara might be a nice change . . . obviously his wife couldn't leave the boutique in the middle of the season, but I had just caught him the day a play he was in had folded. Why not, he said . . . why not . . .

7

It's too bad that the man who killed Doug shortly after our separate return from the Sahara is not able to benefit from what I have written about Dewitt and Doug. Garcia, the man who killed Doug, was taking a leisurely stroll along Broome Street one evening after Doug's and Dewitt's return from Africa, when he caught sight of an attractive and well-dressed couple entering a building on the corner of Broome and Varick. Intuitively, he could tell from their appearance that they lived interesting lives in what must be a well-designed apartment filled with all sorts of intriguing objects they had collected on their travels. A minute after Doug and his wife had entered the building, Garcia, standing on the street below, saw the light go on in their second-floor apartment. He tested the fire escape, and made a mental note of where the building was located, filing it away in his brain for future use.

Garcia is of Spanish descent. Wearing a white raincoat, he stood on Broome Street staring at a second floor window.

Why on earth is Garcia wearing a white raincoat?

Isn't it conspicuous, Garcia? Juanita, his common-law wife asked him. Won't people remember seeing you in the white raincoat? She is lying on a Castro convertible reading a Spanish magazine, while Garcia is sharpening his knife. Most of the things that are advertised in Spanish and in American magazines are on view in their crowded four-room apartment. Shortly after I returned from the desert I met a man in a bar on Fourteenth Street who wore a white raincoat. When I close my eyes I can see the interior of the bar, and the white raincoat hanging from a hook on the wall near the bar entrance. I no longer recall the man's name.

8

Each evening Garcia carefully and thoughtfully sharpens his knife. Juanita no longer asks him where he is going. He takes a subway downtown. Just like everyone else Garcia uses public transportation. He drops a token into the slot, and walks through the turnstile. He is wearing a conspicuous white raincoat, but no one pays any attention. Like everyone else, Garcia has his preferences. He prefers the D train to the F train, the *News* to the *Post*, the West Side to the East Side. He presses his knife against Doug's throat because he finds it difficult to rely solely on language. Language constricts. Yet, when it came to the showdown between Doug and Garcia, Garcia spoke up, wasting a valuable second or two, saying: Now I must hurt you, or words to that effect.

By and large, it would seem to me that Garcia's prior successes had always been predicated on his heightened awareness of the obstacles he might encounter in the dark interior of each apartment he entered. Before leaving for the Sahara, I too tried to familiarize myself with the obstacles I might encounter, to lessen the danger that lay ahead, although, by bringing Doug and Dewitt together, I did not diminish the difficulties of the trip, I increased them drastically.

By entering an apartment through the window, Garcia has deprived himself of the welcome he would most likely receive if he were to use a more orthodox entry. I didn't know of Garcia's existence until one morning a few weeks after my return from the Sahara I picked up the *Times* and saw on one of the back pages a small photograph of Doug next to a photograph of Garcia. They were both exceedingly handsome men. One had carried a knife, the other a loaded pistol. In a sense they were a well matched pair. When questioned by the police, I said that I hadn't heard a sound, being a deep sleeper.

PART TWO

1

Doug and I ran into Dewitt in the desert near Bordj Violette, which is quite close to the Erg Iguidi and only some hundred and fifty miles northwest of the Chenachane Oasis. At first, caught off guard, I felt terribly embarrassed. All along I had hoped we would not run into him. I had carefully planned this trip to the Erg Iguidi, knowing that Dewitt was traveling in the opposite direction. Why he should at the last moment have changed his plan is still not clear to me. Had I known that we would encounter Dewitt in the Sahara I would have unhesitatingly postponed the trip. I certainly would not have asked Doug to join me. Where exactly are you planning to go, Doug had asked me. Oh, I'm not certain . . . I was deliberately vague. I preferred instead to speak of the splendor of the desert. I suppose I was simply repeating what Dewitt had told me. By this time I discovered that Doug had met Dewitt. They had met a week or so prior to Dewitt's departure. But they weren't friends. I still don't know who introduced them. At any rate, Dewitt, in a fit of pique, pretended not to recognize Doug, and I was compelled to make the introductions. Doug? Doug? said Dewitt, staring blankly at Doug. Of course, poor Doug had no way of knowing that Dewitt had invited me to accompany him on this trip. The problem, as I saw it, was that I had been unable to come to a decision, and by the time I did, it was too late. Dewitt had already left. Had left, I might add, without even saying good-by. I still remember the overwhelming relief when I was told he had gone. All the same I knew I had behaved badly, and in attempting to obliterate my action, or rather my lack of action, from my mind, I found myself repeatedly telling all my friends what had happened. I was somewhat startled by the uniformity of their response, which at first I put down to the way I was presenting the story. The way I was distorting what had taken place to make my own position appear as favorable as possible. But it later occurred to me that this wasn't necessarily so, and that perhaps their response was absolutely genuine. But why do you keep saying that you envy me? I asked them. Because Dewitt invited you to accompany him. There! They had finally said it. But I still didn't know what to make of it. On the one hand I was sincerely pleased by what they had said, since it indicated that Dewitt must have thought a lot of me. After all, Dewitt had a great many friends, more friends than I have, yet I was the only one he had invited to accompany him. On the other hand I was extremely disturbed by the implication of my irresponsible behavior. If only I had called Dewitt before he left for the desert.

2

For the past few days I haven't been myself. It's nothing tangible. I don't even have a fever. Again Dewitt and Doug are enthusiastically making all kinds of plans for tomorrow while I remain lying on the cot in the tent. For some inexplicable reason I find their proximity intensely annoying. I went to the desert on the spur of the moment, in order to have a closer look at it, in order to experience its vastness, in order to see at first hand the terrain that Dewitt wanted to explore.

3

Initially Dewitt made it clear that the two of us were an unexpected annoyance. He had just begun to adjust himself to being alone with the Bedouins and the vast emptiness of the desert. Hardly giving us time to catch our breath he asked us to leave. To get the hell out . . . but then relented somewhat when I explained that we were almost out of water and running short of gasoline. During the next few days it occurred to me that in the past we had never had much to say to each other, but in the city, filled with the noise of people coming and going, this lack of communication seemed somehow less noticeable than now, crowded together as we were under one roof, in one car, while the emptiness around us only served to accentuate the silence. Sullenly I retreated into myself, retreated into the tiny oasis where we were staying. While Doug and Dewitt formalized their new friendship by cheerfully poring over maps, or trying to repair our Land Rover, I rested in the shade of one of the palm trees that surround our campsite, and wrote letters to my friends.

4

Dewitt and I had a few friends in common, and naturally, so did Doug and I; however, they were not the same friends, therefore whenever I spoke about a mutual friend with Dewitt or Doug, one or the other was excluded from the conversation. I was not trying to act divisively. I simply cannot go on for hours about magnificent sunsets, lizards, scorpions, cactus, partly because I don't have an eye for such things. Consequently, whenever I had something to say, I seemed to make one or the other extremely irritable. This in turn caused the acute throbbing in my left shoulder, yet, throughout I managed to keep my self-control, and to keep smiling at the Bedouins. I also smiled at Dewitt and Doug, although all this smiling made my facial muscles ache severely. In turn both Dewitt and Doug smiled back at me, but I could detect a profound lack of sincerity in their response.

5

In the morning I would prepare the coffee, in the evening I would light the lantern. I had a few other chores, but I must admit that they were equally insignificant. It took me three weeks to realize how different I was from Doug and Dewitt. I lacked their self-deprecating sense of humor, their exaggerated sense of fair play, their at times incredible patience, as well as their innate politeness. Unlike me, both of them were simply bursting with good humor and tact. Being in their company made me wonder why Dewitt had invited me in the first place. It was the most puzzling aspect of the journey. I now believe that it was the reason why I had set out for the Sahara. I still couldn't come up with a convincing reason. It seemed clear to me that Dewitt should have asked Doug to join him instead of asking me. And it is more than likely that Dewitt, had he known Doug a bit better, would have asked him instead of me. But then again, one can never tell. I might, for all I know, have led Dewitt to believe that I was the person he wanted to be with on this trip. Clearly, in some way, I had passed a test without even knowing that I was taking it.

6

Dewitt and Doug got along splendidly. It was Doug's first trip to the desert, but unlike me he adapted himself at once to its discomforts. He loved the Bedouins, the locusts, the foul-tasting water, moreover, he excelled as a cook, a driver, a mechanic, and was a first-rate shot, in addition to being an excellent mimic, and an altogether amusing companion. When we first met, Doug told Dewitt, you firmly pressed my hand and said, I wouldn't be at all surprised if we run into each other in the near future. Dewitt laughed uproariously. Yes, Doug was all right, with his incredible memory, his pleasant smile, his witty remarks, his handsome face, and his physical endurance. I always felt that if we should by some mishap get stuck in the Erg Iguidi, Doug would keep on going until he reached Marrakech, a thousand miles away. He was indestructible, it seemed to me at that time.

7

Each evening Doug and Dewitt played several hands of gin rummy. Naturally I was asked to join in. It was taken for granted that I would, yet when I didn't that first time, I was never asked again. I suppose I could have sat down with them and joined the game. Possibly they never gave it a second thought. Perhaps they believed that I didn't play cards. It is of no consequence, yet I must admit, it still rankles slightly.

8

On my return I promptly informed everyone that Dewitt and Doug, my former friends and companions, had abandoned me after stealing my dictionary and a couple of hundred dollars in cash. They took the dictionary and the cash while I was asleep. I told my friends that I didn't really mind losing all that hard-earned money, but without the dictionary I felt quite lost in the desert.

For one thing, it impeded my letter writing. After Doug and Dewitt had left in the Land Rover, leaving me in possession of the other badly damaged car, I spent three months in the oasis surviving on dates and some canned artichoke hearts until I managed to get a ride back to Marrakech with a French surveyor. The Bedouins, whenever we stopped, were unfailingly kind and hospitable. Now that I wanted to run into Dewitt and Doug there was absolutely no likelihood of my doing so. Still, the trip was not a total loss. Without Dewitt and Doug I felt more relaxed. Each morning as I climbed one of the fifty-foot date trees, I found myself cheerfully singing at the top of my lungs. On an impulse, after my return, I rang Doug's doorbell. I didn't really know what I was going to say. I think I just wanted an explanation for his odd behavior. I was quite calm as I waited for Doug to answer the door. But Doug didn't answer the door, his wife did. She stared at me as if amazed to see me standing at their door. What on earth do you want now? I explained that I had just returned. I'll tell Doug that you called, she said. I couldn't understand the barely controlled venom in her voice. If anything, I considered myself the damaged party. On that inconclusive note, I returned to my apartment. It occured to me that she was angry because she had been excluded from my invitation to Doug. Still, I was confident that the next time I ran into Doug we would straighten out our misunderstanding. Although I couldn't bring myself to admit it to my friends, I had found the missing cash in the lining of my sleeping bag. But there was no trace of the dictionary . . .

A month later I ran into Dewitt on the street. We said hello, and stopped to speak. I don't recall who stopped first. It may have been I. We also shook hands, and I noticed that the hand he held out was quite limp. I must say I was startled by his limp hand. I racked my brains to remember if his hand had been limp on the previous occasions when we had shaken hands. It also occurred to me that he might be trying to convey something by his peculiar handshake. I just couldn't fathom what it might be. It was an awkward meeting. Both of us were tense. I more so than he. I was curious if he would apologize for lifting my dictionary. But he didn't refer to it. Only after we had parted did I remember that I had neglected to ask him about Doug. A friend of mine recently met Doug. Doug spoke about our trip to the Sahara, strongly implying that I could not distinguish fact from fancy.

9

Each time Garcia slides open a window and enters an apartment a familiar list of objects is instantly identified, one by one, thereby clarifying his next move. Implicit in the mechanics of the entry is the need to situate and locate the self in relation to all other surfaces in the dark interior. Having made his entry, Garcia permits the chair to lead him to the table, the cord to the lamp, the desk top to the smooth marble paperweight. In the dark each object gradually reveals its outlines to the language of the brain. Garcia wears sneakers to deaden the sound of his footsteps. He walks as if he was crossing an endless desert . . . vast, empty stretches of space separating unseen obstacles. Entering an apartment by means of the window is simply another way of shopping. By the time Doug felt a slight movement disturb the air at the side of his face, it was too late. The signal of alarm reached Doug's brain a split second after he had opened his eyes. In order to assess what had happened, Doug followed the outlines of the bed, as if by tracing in his mind the object upon which he was lying he could determine who he was, and what he was doing in this bed at this very moment. Trying to solve this problem became the greatest obstacle as Garcia pressed the point of his knife against Doug's throat.

10

A day later I read in *The New York Times* how Garcia entered the next-door apartment. Like most shoppers he had developed a discriminating taste. Perhaps, like me on my return from the desert, he had expected Doug and his wife to be away somewhere, spending July and August on the Cape or in East Hampton. By the time Doug's ear picked up a strange sound at the side of his bed, it was decidedly too late. Methodically Garcia tied Doug's hands behind his back with the lamp cord. However, Doug was in fine shape after his trip to the desert, and in no time untied his hands, and during Garcia's brief absence from the bedroom made a dash for the closet.

Doug was always well dressed. He once confided to me that he bought his suits and jackets secondhand. There's a fantastic place near Canal Street, he said, where one can get the most incredible buys. His tan double-breasted blazer was hanging next to his brown double-breasted blazer in the bedroom closet. Garcia had looked into the closet, but Garcia wasn't shopping for a blazer, and overlooked the slight bulge in the right-hand pocket of the tan blazer. Had he spotted it he might not later have found himself staring down the barrel of Doug's .38 when he returned to the bedroom where he had left Doug tied up on the bed. Doug's wife, who had been made to accompany Garcia to the next room, also stood in the doorway staring at Doug. Perhaps, ever so briefly, Doug also stared at himself. As a professional actor and model, he was bound to have a heightened awareness of his actions. The initial surprise and advantage rested with Doug, and yet . . .

I will always remember Doug in his tan blazer standing on the corner of Broome waiting for his wife. After what had happened I fully expected that she would move out of the apartment. But she hasn't.

NON-SITE

1

This is an introduction to Mr. Bert Eon's generosity. It is also a story of a friendship and a great love. The few landscapes that have been included are all framed and hanging on the walls of Mr. Bert Eon's home and office. Since Mr. Bert Eon's visit I am no longer concerned about the paper. All the arrangements have been made, and the paper is provided for. Of course, I am grateful to Mr. Bert Eon for his support. Without him the weekly would never be mailed to its 4,758 subscribers. Without him . . . but enough said. The last time Mr. Bert Eon came to see me he was thirty-nine. He thoughtfully looked at the peeling paint on my walls, at the deplorable conditions of my workroom, at the ink stains on my hands, and shook his head sadly. This will have to change, he said. This will simply have to change. He carefully selected a chair to sit on. He lowered his bulk. One brief moment of panic. Just another incident in my life.

Largely as a result of my candor and solicitude, Mr. Bert Eon stayed in my office for several hours. He was younger then, and had the stamina, and possibly, although this is pure speculation, also the curiosity. It was curiosity, I'm convinced, that impelled him to assist me with a weekly supply of paper and to cover all my other expenses, including the cost of mailing the 4,758 copies.

But I also have to thank my friend Mr. George Ol for introducing me to Mr. Bert Eon, and the considerable pressure on my behalf that was put on Mr. Bert Eon by his wife must also be taken into account. I am of two minds about Mr. Bert Eon. Don't you admire his wit? George asked me. Yes, I admire his wit and his expensive Italian suits. The suits he wears produce in me a kind of euphoric reverie that comes close to envy. I can still see Mr. Bert Eon in his well-pressed dark suit and white silk shirt, carefully stretching out his legs, and resting his feet on my cluttered desk. I say, he said, his face wreathed in a beatific smile, would you mind wiping the tips of my shoes . . . ? Just the tip . . . Yes . . . that's it. I felt no humiliation, no sense of degradation at all, because service is second nature to me. After all, what's the difference between putting out a small-town newspaper and wiping the shoes of the man I respect . . .

Mr. Bert Eon was thirty-nine at the time. Today he is considerably older. At least five years have passed. I do not keep track of the years, only of the weeks . . . I age weekly as I try to meet the schedule . . . try to leave as few blank spaces as possible in the paper . . . Now that my secretary is gone, everything takes twice as long. How can anyone expect me to do all the work by myself. Of course, it happens to be the life I love. I could not envision a different sort of existence, although, if it came to that, I am as fit as the next man. I could do a variety of things . . . I could even become a painter and join the group who daily stand with their long ladders at the corner of Grand and Dexter, waiting to be hired . . . They are a friendly group. But the daily inhalation of all those toxic fumes has left its mark on their pasty faces. Faces that are not strikingly different from my own. You could be taken for a painter, one of the men once told me. That is why I mention it. I even wrote about the men. I interviewed them at work. Afterward I was disappointed not to hear any of them mention the article, but then they probably do not pick up a copy of my paper, or, out of a natural and understandable shyness, they kept silent, fearful that in their total innocence they might say something inappropriate. Still, they remain friendly, inasmuch as anyone is still friendly. Good morning, Mr. Nap, they say as I pass. I know they are critical of me because I don't loiter in the square. Because I don't roll up the sleeves of my shirt and reveal for all the world to see the absence of those naked frolicking ladies that they carry around on their forearms. I am inclined to stop and tell them that their gallon-size cans of paint are inconveniencing the passers-by . . . But actually no one objects. The other day I tripped over a tarp someone had left lying on the street. I know they resent my not having my office painted. If they give me sufficient reason, I shall write about them again.

Although a town this size can hardly support six painters, there must be over a dozen standing on the street daily. A dozen create a glut on the market. It may be the reason why they have become surly. Still, they too have their festive days, their annual Painters' Festival. People from all over come to Grand and Dexter on that day to observe the Dance of the Ladders . . . those tall unwieldly ladders which they lean against the corner building at Dexter and Grand.

2

George Ol complains that my paper is too bleak. That it is devoid of those little things that enable one to endure the long, long silence of each evening.

And how is Mrs. Eon? I ask him. How is she doing?

George Ol enters the office, a little out of breath. He's the only person I can depend on for news. Very little goes unnoticed by George Ol.

Listen, says George Ol, I've just seen the most curious thing . . . He is holding his side, and making the most comical grimaces . . . Really, I do not find it in my heart to dislike George Ol. George and I have known each other for quite some time. We are nodding acquaintances who speak to each other . . . at one time we shared an apartment and Gloria. It was not the most convenient arrangement by any means, but he had the apartment and I had Gloria. She was my secretary. My former secretary. She was one of the first women . . . that is to say the first who let me, and afterward . . . God knows, the arrangement was not one of those contractually binding agreements. She permitted George . . . she kept shuttling back and forth between our respective rooms . . . It had its drawbacks, but for want of anything better . . . I could not find another apartment, and he, although this is a supposition, could not find another woman willing to . . . or perhaps George is a bit of a queer, liking a woman that belongs to another man. I would not put it past him. Gloria was a superb typist. I could depend on her. That dour expression on her face was, I suspect, meant to discourage others, or to dispel any suspicion that she . . . oh well . . . so there was George, Gloria, and myself. We could have continued for years. I mean, what was there to stop our hesitant, almost furtive fornication . . . I think that George's presence in the adjacent room imbued our lovemaking with a certain liveliness that it had lacked before. Anyhow, Gloria's gone. And so's the apartment, of course. Still, George Ol and I see each other regularly . . . and Gloria, efficient, irreplaceable Gloria is working for Mr. Bert Eon. George has told me that she now has a sparkle in her eyes . . . I suppose I could have held on to Gloria. I discussed the matter with George five years ago. What do you think, George? George has a fine, detached mind when it comes to matters that touch on business. What do I do? Mr. Bert Eon has been looking at my office. He intends to finance the paper. I took him on a tour of the office. I showed him all my chairs, the typewriters, the cabinet where I keep all my supplies . . . During his visit he happened, or rather his eyes happened on Gloria. She wasn't looking her best by any means . . . but I caught him looking at her legs, and then his gaze drifted up . . . but chiefly, his eyes lingered on her legs. My heart was beating frantically . . . You've got a pretty run-down place, Mr. Bert Eon had complained. We manage, I said brightly. We manage, Gloria and I . . .

Does she let you? he asked.

Well, there I was caught in a bind. Do I or don't I. Is it to my advantage to tell him or should I keep my mouth shut. At moments like this one tries desperately to think of some precedent. Anyhow . . . I did, and I didn't. I believe I smirked. Well, what's she like? Mr. Bert Eon asked. This only made matters worse. She was my sole experience . . . so I smirked again.

It's incredible, shouted George Ol. It's absolutely incredible . . . the painters are standing around without their ladders . . .

What? I looked sharply at him, but he was serious. No levity, no sign of amusement on his face. So we ran to Dexter and Grand just in time to see the painters climb on the back of a truck and drive off. The truck contained their cans of paint and their tarpaulins, but not a single ladder. I counted at least sixteen men.

Take notes, said George excitedly.

Oh shit, are you going to tell me how to run my business?

3

George stands in the living room. He is feeling a slight bit restless.
He is also feeling a slight bit under the weather. He hasn't seen
Vivian for a few days. She has made herself inaccessible to him . . .
He understands nothing of her private vision. He is still mesmerized
by the complexity of this household . . . by, to take only one example, the efficient way the laundry delivers all their clean linen and
Mr. Bert Eon's silk shirts and underwear and handkerchiefs, with
all the information marked on a longish slip of paper which is
attached with a pin to the neatly wrapped package. One glance at
the slip of paper listing what is neatly folded inside the package is
enough to dispel the gloom for an entire day . . .

George intends to mention the missing ladders. He can hardly
contain his excitement. I am hoping that Vivian will ask her husband, Mr. Bert Eon, about it. Clarifications of some sort are bound
to follow . . .

4

This is an introduction to Vivian's watch. Swiss timepiece, of course,
with an attractive gold chain-link bracelet. She glances at it peri-
odically, measuring the depth of her anger . . . no, her irritation.
Vivian is too controlled to feel any anger. Anger would be too difficult to hide all these years. Mr. Bert Eon is aware of her irritation.
He smoothes the wrinkles of her irritation with his hairy hand, and
says: It's all right. If you wish to spend a week end at the seashore,
we can drive out this Friday as soon as I return from the office. But
this only aggravates the situation, since she wishes to be at the
seashore with someone else. Someone more refined, someone
younger and more glamorous. But she accepts his suggestion with
bad grace . . . So it goes . . . Thank you, dear. He looks at her un-
suspectingly. He glares at the man from U. P. The delivery man
announces the name of the store and pockets the tip Vivian had
slipped him . . .

George is privy to this and much more. He is privy to the efficient way the household is run. George has no household to speak
of. But he can appreciate the complexities of a household. The

177

cleaning, vacuuming, heating, drying, polishing, waxing that goes on uninterruptedly.

5

This an introduction to George's eye. It is also an introduction to the smoothness, the perfect smoothness of a white Formica table top. A few descriptions of rather bleak landscapes are also included, but without exception they are all framed and hanging in the over-furnished living room of Mr. and Mrs. Bert Eon. Not ˙that the exterior world is without bleakness, but the eye cannot recognize it, since the bleakness isn't framed . . . At least not that particular eye, or, rather, pair of eyes . . .

George has a fine eye for detail. It helps him assess, so to speak, the enormity of his envy. It also enables him to ingest the nuances, the fleshy nuances of Vivian's crossed legs, and permits him to examine the flawless line of her nape as she leans forward to study the design of her carpet. George stations himself in the doorway to keep track of the inflow and outflow of Mr. Bert Eon's acquisitions. He is doing this for the sake of his observant eye.

The most one can ever hope to describe is a kind of insecurity of vision, as people madly rush from one location to the next, scratching their names into trees, walls, and all garden furniture, as well as other equally harmless inoffensive utilitarian objects that happen briefly to catch their eyes.

Mr. Bert Eon is like everyone else at forty-four, except that he's tougher, louder, and hairier. He has accepted George's presence in the same way that he has accepted the inevitable piano in the living room, namely, with resignation. Mr. Bert Eon fills the entire day with his energetic activities . . . which indicate a perseverance and a single-mindedness that George does not possess. George puts the blame on his eyes. They are so selective . . . they take such pleasure in seeing the joyful reunion of colors and the assembly of a bouquet of irises, a floral tribute to Vivian's beauty.

She brushes her long hair. Somehow, it is a familiar picture. She stands in front of the oval mirror admiring herself. This is an intro-duction to Vivian's body. How many men have stared at her with longing. How many men have been attracted by the clean but slightly acrid taste of her body and spirit. She avoids meeting their glances and thus protects her body from the pitfalls of desire. At night she beds with Mr. Bert Eon, but as far as she's concerned she's simply covering herself with an old scratchy blanket. Each evening she selects from her extensive wardrobe what she will wear the following day. Her choice, arrived at after considerable hesitation, indicates the degree to which she is prepared to submit her white skin to the naked stare of men.

This is an introduction to Vivian's second watch. It is also a Swiss timepiece. Quite elegant, with a crocodile leather strap. She glances at it, measuring her distress . . . measuring the time that will elapse before someone will carry her off to the hotel at the seashore.

6

This is an introduction to the color blue. It so happens that George's eyes are blue. While crossing the street on his way to visit Vivian a speck of dust was lodged in his left eye. There was one brief moment of panic, as George, pressing a handkerchief to the afflicted eye, crossed over to the other side of the street, and narrowly missed being hit by a car. It occured to him that he could have been killed, or at least maimed for life.

While taking tea with Vivian, he describes his day. It is a perfectly ordinary sort of day. Uneventful except for one incident. As usual, he stares longingly at Vivian. He yearns for her. He listens to the radio. They drink their tea. The sun is shining. Why don't we sit in the garden? he suggests. She agrees. Mr. Bert Eon comes home at six. He left his office earlier than usual. He is in robust health and feeling very pleased with himself. He is now in his forties. He pours himself a drink . . . George observes that Bert as usual has failed to offer him a drink. He decides to overlook the slight.

At eleven, Mr. Bert Eon and his wife go to bed. Bert is still feeling pleased with himself. Consequently, he's amused by everything his wife says. George was nearly run over today, she remarks. He roars with laughter. She sits in front of the oval mirror combing her hair. Perhaps she is postponing the moment when she will crawl into bed with Mr. Bert Eon. But this is doubtful. How was your day? she inquires. But Mr. Bert Eon has fallen asleep. He has fallen asleep despite the bright light overhead. Nervously, she picks up a novel.

7

This is an introduction to the ladders. They are still missing. The painters left in a truck four days ago. The driver drove along 14A as far as Grant's, then turned left. He could be anywhere by now. The ladders are stored in the local fire station. The firemen tried to conceal them from me. They tried to distract my attention from the ladders. But they are not very practiced at this sort of deception. I was able to count the ladders and, later, able to confirm their absence from the homes of the painters. What this means I cannot say.

This is also a story about a friendship and a great but frustrated love. The few landscapes that have been included are framed and hanging from the walls of Mr. Bert Eon's offices. Most of the walls remain inaccessible to me. All I've ever received is a brief description of the walls and landscapes. Vivian, when she isn't reading novels in bed, is redecorating Mr. Bert Eon's many offices. She orders paint by the barrel, and truckloads of wallpaper. At night, the guard at the elevator has seen her slip into the building wearing only a sheer nightgown. Barefoot she races up and down the empty corridors, trying to decide what everything would look like if it were painted another color. Despite George's unfailing eye, she doesn't ask him for advice. She feels he doesn't deserve her respect, because he has never allowed his adoration for her to interfere with his daily routine.

8

This is an introduction to Mr. Bert Eon's feet, which he is resting on top of his new desk as he reads the latest report from his engineer in Missouri. The engineer is writing on the firm's stationery. He describes the estuary and the magnificent sunset. It is evident that the letter has been written for Mr. Bert Eon's amusement. The engineer, a man named Bud, recognizes Mr. Bert Eon's weakness. Everyone in Mr. Eon's office has at one time or another encountered his polished black shoes. They are a boundary of sorts. They enclose the lower extremities of this man. They are black and always shined to a high gloss. Mr. Bert Eon's feet are also resting on several reports that are scattered on the polished surface of his desk. The feet are resting on a surface generally reserved for the hands. The feet inspire everyone in the office with a feeling of helplessness. Wipe my shoes, Mr. Bert Eon will say. Open my zip please, Mr. Bert Eon will say. Gloria, please call my wife and tell her not to expect me for dinner.

Physically, Gloria does not resemble Mr. Bert Eon's wife. Both, however, are known to read novels. They may have met on one occasion in a library. Since Gloria cannot read novels during the day, she reads them at night.

This is an introduction to Gloria's skirt, which has been draped over the back of a chair, while she, dressed in her blouse and panties, takes dictation. Dear Bud, Mr. Bert Eon dictates in a flat voice. Received your letter of Tuesday the third. You lucky devil, being able to breathe the unpolluted Missouri air. He continues in this vein, not neglecting to mention that his wife had run into Bud's attractive wife the day before. Absent-mindedly, he stares at the half-undressed secretary, while his thoughts are on Bud's smooth-skinned wife . . . He doesn't know the precise relationship that exists between Bud and his wife. But he can detect a flirtatiousness in Bud's wife that is different from the antiseptic flirtatiousness of his own wife. In his letter he sows the seeds of suspicion. He enjoys doing this to Bud. His secretary smiles timidly. Her timid smile is like a thin crack in the bathroom ceiling that has been covered with plaster. Despite all attempts to hide it, the crack remains in evidence.

Mr. Bert Eon's nakedness reinforces the image of the robust health he enjoys. His body challenges the smooth nakedness of his wife and of his secretary. They are repelled and also terribly attracted to him. Kissing him is like chewing hairs . . .

First, I touched her hand lightly, Mr. Bert Eon told George. She displayed the traits one has come to associate with ambivalence. She was torn between wanting to move her hand away from mine and wanting to leave her hand where it was. This turmoil, only hinted at, and by no means verifiable, made me in turn evince a hasty and somewhat unconvincing interest in her upper regions . . . to take her mind off my hand . . . so to speak, ha ha.

He's a bit of a shit with women, George confided to me. All the same George feels flattered to have been taken into Mr. Bert Eon's confidence.

9

This is an introduction to a damaged rear axle. The truck is parked in a garage. It bears an out-of-town license. The driver is chatting with a mechanic. At the same time that they are sharing certain experiences, they are also withholding others. The one experience the driver is glad to share with the mechanic is the Dance of the Ladders. The driver is trying to persuade the mechanic to repair his truck by Friday, because he has to get back in time for the Painters' Festival.

The engineer is holed up in a motel writing another letter to Mr. Bert Eon. In it he describes a slight accident that had occurred when his car was hit by a truck carrying a group of painters. Fortunately, he escaped injury, but his Pontiac was a complete loss. The Pontiac was a company car. The engineer chooses his words carefully. The sun is setting by the time he finishes his letter.

Mr. Bert Eon is also a Presidential Adviser on Bridges and Tunnels. So far he's been in the red oval room and Jefferson's closet at the White House. Vivian and George are kept informed. George Ol cannot cease to wonder at the large quantity of food Mr. Bert Eon, his wife Vivian, and their children manage to consume daily. The children have names and lead separate lives. They are not fazed by the bleak landscapes in the living room. They are blind to so many things. George Ol doesn't know what to say to them.

10

This is an introduction to a muffled groan and an unmade bed, and a pair of laddered stockings lying on the floor. The muffled groan is music to the ears of Mr. Bert Eon. He does everything in his power to induce Bud's wife to repeat the delightful sound. But there are times when Mr. Bert Eon comes to a stop. Or, rather, there are times when he is made aware of his own immobility. This may come about in the following manner: Mr. Bert Eon finds himself pensively staring at a windowpane. To another person it may appear that Mr. Bert Eon is simply staring at the lawn, or at his neighbor's house, or at his slim wife Vivian, who is nervously crossing or uncrossing her slim legs. But Mr. Bert Eon is simply staring at the glass. He is depressed by the property of glass . . . perhaps it also confounds him, as only it should.

Vivian, on the other hand, is so immersed in the novel she is reading that everything else, including the distant sound of a muffled groan, is only an intrusion. The books she reads all have a beginning, a middle, and an end. She is satisfied that life follows the dictates of the novels she reads. Glass to her is positively attractive, as long as it isn't smeared.

11

This is an introduction to next week's headline. It is in 72-point Futura Medium Condensed. It covers the upper third of the front page. It announces the Painters' Festival at Dexter and Grand. There is no mention of the absent painters and no mention of the hidden ladders. The article is filled with encouraging news. The ladies' auxiliary club will serve refreshments.

The letter from Mr. Bert Eon arrives on Monday. It contains a check covering all my expenses, as well as some useful information which he would like to have me print. The information consists of a list of thirty new employees, and a four-line mention of Bud Glue, who is on an assignment in Missouri. It is common knowledge that Bud Glue has been sent there to give Mr. Bert Eon a free hand with Bud's wife, Charleen Glue.

Meanwhile, Vivian dreams of romance. She reads novels because they help her organize her life. Her friend George is always around observing the activities of the household.

There's not enough room for all of us in this life, said Vivian. I received her hysterical phone call the day after Bud returned. During Bud's absence, his wife has mysteriously acquired a new car. She also has switched to a more expensive dry cleaner. Bud runs his eyes down the list from the dry cleaner. Since when do we send our sheets to be laundered? he asks his wife. But he is a practical man. He absorbs all kinds of information. Undressing his wife, he absorbs the information of her expensive underwear.

12

This is a final salute to George's eye. The eye is the key to the troubled adding machine in George's head. This is also an introduction to the smooth surface, the marvelous, smooth, unmarred surface of the white, shiny Formica counter which serves as a bar in the living room. A few descriptions of somewhat bleak, desolate, and inhospitable landscapes are also included. But without exception these landscapes are the product of third or fourth-rate early nineteenth-century talent. The eye keeps returning to the white Formica because it stands out. The perfect world of Formica, thinks George. It is an agreeable surface.

I've just shot Bert, said Vivian on the phone. I wanted you to be the first to know. There's great excitement in the town because the painters haven't returned, and tomorrow is the Dance of the Ladders.

NOTE: *"Non-Sites" was the title of an exhibition of earth projects by Robert Smithson at the Dwan Gallery in February 1969.*—W.A.